Christoph...

Turning in... ...welling

Poems

Graywolf Press

This publication is made possible, in part, by the voters of Minnesota through a
Minnesota State Arts Board Operating Support grant, thanks to a legislative appropri-
ation from the arts and cultural heritage fund, and through grants from the National
Endowment for the Arts and the Wells Fargo Foundation Minnesota. Significant sup-
port has also been provided by Target, the McKnight Foundation, Amazon.com, and
other generous contributions from foundations, corporations, and individuals. To these
organizations and individuals we offer our heartfelt thanks.

ART WORKS.
arts.gov

MINNESOTA
STATE ARTS BOARD

CLEAN
WATER
LAND &
LEGACY
AMENDMENT

WELLS
FARGO

TARGET.

Across the Mutual Landscape was originally published by Graywolf Press in 1984, as the
winner of the 1983 Walt Whitman Award of the Academy of American Poets, selected
by Michael S. Harper.

Published by Graywolf Press
250 Third Avenue North, Suite 600
Minneapolis, Minnesota 55401

All rights reserved.

www.graywolfpress.org

Published in the United States of America

ISBN 978-1-55597-713-9

2 4 6 8 9 7 5 3 1
First Graywolf Printing, 2015

Library of Congress Control Number: 2014960043

Cover design: Kyle G. Hunter

Cover photo: Karen Durlach

The Graywolf Poetry Re/View Series

No one else sounds quite like Christopher Gilbert (1949–2007), who won the 1983 Walt Whitman Award for *Across the Mutual Landscape*. His voice feels timeless in its immediacy, and the poems startle in their almost uncanny ability to grant readers access to a mind at work. Though his book became a quiet yet central influence for a generation of African-American poets, Gilbert never published another. This volume includes a second manuscript, brilliantly ahead of its time. Together they make a powerful case for a poet of remarkable presence.

Mark Doty, Series Editor

The Graywolf Poetry Re/View Series brings essential books of contemporary American poetry back into the light of print. Each volume—chosen by series editor Mark Doty—is introduced by a poet who comes to the work with a passionate admiration. The Graywolf Poetry Re/View Series offers all-but-lost masterworks of recent American poetry to a new generation of readers.

Volumes in the Graywolf Poetry Re/View Series:
   Collected Poems by Lynda Hull,
      with an introduction by Yusef Komunyakaa
   Letters to a Stranger by Thomas James,
      with an introduction by Lucie Brock-Broido
   The Salt Ecstasies by James L. White,
      with an introduction by Mark Doty
   Turning into Dwelling by Christopher Gilbert,
      with an introduction by Terrance Hayes

Contents

CHRIS GILBERT: AN IMPROVISATION
(Music of the Striving That Was There)

III. Into the Into

Introduction

> At closing time
> standing outside the public library
> with ID card expired,
> the books remain on shelves—
> Lev Vygotsky, Toni Morrison, Levertov, Cassirer,
> and the Zora Neale Hurston (which probably isn't there) . . .

"Who is this Christopher Gilbert and why am I only just hearing about him?" That's what I continue to ask myself at almost every encounter with this poet. Typing the opening stanza of "The 'The,'" for example, I lingered again on the authors named in the poem. I had to research Lev Vygotsky and Ernst Cassirer. Part of the wink in those opening lines is that the speaker (someone so like Christopher Gilbert we could call him Christopher Gilbert) is also planning to research the authors. In seeing what the seeker seeks we see something of the seeker. The poem tells us something about his eclectic intelligence as well as his eclectic curiosity. He's after Lev Vygotsky, the Russian development psychologist who wrote in 1934 that "thought does not express itself in words, but rather realizes itself in them," and Ernst Cassirer, the neo-Kantian German philosopher who wrote in 1929 that "the human spirit in astonishing delusion flees from itself while seeking itself." The other writers, Denise Levertov, Toni Morrison, and Zora Neale Hurston, also suggest a great deal about the poetics of this poet: political, lyrical, anthropological. But again part of the poem's genius is Gilbert is also looking to learn something about himself: his poetics, his personhood.

Finding he has no access he can only say how it feels to be someone *like* Christopher Gilbert:

> I feel like some third person
> locked outside the language
> through which I am
> the things I mean.

How can one be introduced to a poet if not through the poet's poems? How, after encountering such strange brilliance, should one honor a poet who insists, "i am absolutely the I in the writing"? What I did was write an exasperated email to my poetry mentors, pals, and peers asking: "Who is this Christopher Gilbert and why am I only just hearing about him?" Nearly everyone recalled Christopher Gilbert. He'd published a book thirty years ago and vanished.

I first heard of him in 2010 during a walk with a poet beside a lake in rural Maine. "Do you know Chris Gilbert's work," Fran Quinn asked one night at Robert Bly's Great Mother Conference. I was there teaching a poetry workshop, but as the name implies (officially "The Great Mother and New Father Conference"), it is far from your run of the mill poetry gathering. There had been, since its 1975 inception, more than a few occasions for its Jungians, storytellers, activists, dancers, tabla drummers, shamanic astrologers, and poets to weep at the state of the cosmos or the sound of a sitar or the great figure of Bly crossing a rustic threshold. Fran had been there since the very beginning, teaching poetry and watching his friends dazzle and age. I'm half joking when I say I might have been only the third or fourth black dude to have ever attended. We'd been talking about Etheridge Knight, who'd attended the conference in its early years and whose name I first heard from Fran when I was eighteen years old and he was a visiting poet at my small South Carolina college. After twenty years we were meeting for only the second time, and he was somehow introducing me to a second magnificent black poet.

"No," or "I don't know," I said to Fran when he asked if I knew Chris Gilbert's work. Gilbert had once driven to the conference to visit Knight. He'd been a member of Knight's Free People's Poetry Workshops in the eighties when Knight lived in Massachusetts. Gilbert was a great poet, Fran said with his hallmark passion. He had published one book, *Across the Mutual Landscape*, in the early eighties. There was a second manuscript, but Gilbert had died before it could be published. Maybe Fran wiped his nose as he spoke, cleared his throat. He said he and the poet Mary Fell, they'd also been in a workshop with Gilbert years ago, now had the book and its nine or ten different versions back in Indiana. I don't think I asked to see the unpublished manuscript though he must have offered to send it to me. I told him I would run down *Across the Mutual Landscape*, the first book. I didn't leave the conference with Gilbert in the front of my mind. I was pondering stories I'd heard about Knight's presence at the conference and how Fran was still cheering and teaching so many poets.

I may have forgotten Gilbert had his name not floated my way again less than a week after my return home. The poet Ed Pavlic emailed me "Marking Time," a poem by Christopher Gilbert, a poet he'd long admired. I asked if it was the same Chris Gilbert that Fran had mentioned to me. I asked if the poet was dead. "I'm pretty sure Chris Gilbert is alive and living in Providence," Ed said, adding that he'd been thinking about inviting him down to read at the University of Georgia. After a little poking around online, Ed discovered it was indeed the same Christopher Gilbert. It so happened Ed was in Bloomington, Indiana, teaching at a writers conference. I told him Fran lived nearby in Indianapolis. Could he drive there and get the new manuscript? They set a time to meet.

Forgive me. I've drifted from the realm of introduction into the realm of coincidence, nostalgia, great mothers, new fathers, and, very possibly, the work of ghosts. I should simply say during the one or two weeks it took Ed to get the new manuscript back to Georgia, and to scan and share it with me, I read *Across the Mutual Landscape*. I was overwhelmed, awestruck, saddened. I emailed at least a dozen people passages from his long poem, "Horizontal Cosmology," asking each time: "Who is this Christopher Gilbert and why am I only just hearing about him?" Here are a few lines from "The Facts," part six of "Horizontal Cosmology":

> I forget the magic gourd that fit my hands,
> its shake my feeling of having a heart.
> My face is a mask. Everyone wears it.
> When I take it off there's another face.
> I turn around to you, you this moment
> I have come to empty-handed and not myself.

Across the Mutual Landscape has a dialectical quality that still seems groundbreaking. The title alone of "Listening to Monk's *Mysterioso* I Remember Braiding My Sisters' Hair" announces the ways his poems synthesize family and culture, past and present. A poem like "Time with Stevie Wonder in It" reveals the ways his poems move across multiple narratives linking a single moment to all its surrounding moments:

> If this were just a poem
> there would be a timelessness—
> the punchclock midwest would go on
> ticking, the intervals between ticks
> metaphor for the gap in our lives . . .

The end of his first poem in *Across the Mutual Landscape*, "This Bridge Across," succinctly suggests Gilbert's aim in his poetry: "each moment is a boundary I will throw this bridge across."

In the "The Breathing / in / an Emancipatory Space," an essay Gilbert wrote for the *Painted Bride Quarterly*'s 1988 issue devoted to the work of Etheridge Knight, he provides the only explicit commentary I could find regarding his sense of poetry: "For the poet . . . the startling feeling is how much we—as minds—are in the world rather than apart from it. . . . We are our situations." The remark echoes the quotes I referenced at the beginning of this introduction: Vygotsky's notion that the mind is shaped through language and Cassirer's notion that we paradoxically flee ourselves even when we are seeking ourselves. Gilbert often seems to walk the bridge between what's real and what's possible. In the title poem a speaker (one of the Chris Gilberts we meet everywhere) is out walking his dog when he says to the dog: "Let's be simultaneous . . . because for once we both are beings . . . knowing nothing lives as a foreignness." Later in the poem he says, seeming to merge with the consciousness of the dog: "let's begin by being mutual, . . . I'll be damned / if I don't step down in my neighbors' yards / with my mutt's paw and my situation / whole in the world." In Gilbert's poems the self wanders a world that is not narrative, historical, or personal, but all of these things simultaneously: a situation.

This quality of wandering is even more pronounced in the poems of the second manuscript, titled *Chris Gilbert: An Improvisation (Music of the Striving That Was There)*. In the new work a speaker (someone improvising what it means to be Christopher Gilbert, a philosophical flaneur with a wry, blue disposition) is often wondering and wandering. In "On the Way Back Home" he writes we "go out wandering in our various directions." In "Tourist" he writes:

> I am
> into small steps here—I total the bits of me.
> I have lived in countless places, childless,
> without song, and now no church of time ahead
> behind whose doors one can walk and be
> transformed, enormous, again, and facing the sky.

This self becomes a tourist both displaced and situated in his displacement. Selfhood becomes an act of existential improvisation. Selfhood becomes as fluid and difficult as language. These are not difficult poems, but difficulty is often their subject: the difficulty of the gaps between selves, between being and thinking, between timelessness and time. They strive "to build," as Gilbert writes in the poem "Turning into Dwelling," "this language house . . . this loving which lives outside time." This new collection's title, *Turning into Dwelling*, underscores the ways the self is simultaneously restless and reflective in Gilbert's body of work. His poetry makes "turning" both a motion and an act of transformation, and "dwelling" both a shelter and an act of rumination.

I am still, despite countless readings these last years, being introduced to Christopher Gilbert and his selves. He died at the young age of fifty-seven on July 5, 2007, in Providence, Rhode Island. Graywolf published *Across the Mutual Landscape*, when Michael S. Harper selected it for the 1983 Walt Whitman Award. Harper was one of the first poets I emailed in 2010 to ask about Gilbert. He told me Gilbert had died of an "inherited kidney problem"; that as an undergraduate he'd studied with Robert Hayden at the University of Michigan. Part of me wonders how much Gilbert was shaped by his relationships with Hayden, Harper, and Knight. Gilbert, born in Alabama, was, like Knight, a southern transplant; Gilbert, like Hayden, was raised in industrial Michigan; Gilbert, like Harper, lived much of his adult life in Providence, Rhode Island.

While Gilbert melds the poetics of an austere formalist, a radical jazzman, and a restless bluesman, his work is altogether original, indeterminate, and boundless. Harper said he'd dedicated part of his 1998 Frost Medal lecture to Gilbert and read one of his poems "for remembrance." More of us should have remembered him when he lived. We would not need, so soon, to recover him now. Though there were no other books, he maintained his links to poetry and poets, at least through the eighties.

In 1986, after receiving a National Endowment for the Arts fellow-
ship in poetry, he took the year off and was poet-in-residence
at the Robert Frost Place in Franconia, New Hampshire, as well
as a visiting poet at the University of Pittsburgh. "Contemporary
Authors Online Biography Resource Center" cites Gilbert ex-
plaining how the time off was necessary for his poems: "I feel
that my own ability to write poetry wants this; it wants its expe-
rience to be grounded in the firsthand world gained through con-
tact with lives and people, with me—as subject—as an empathy,
with a reflection toward one's deeper and longer life, with goals,
with a concept of use."

The penultimate section of "Into the Into," the last poem in
Chris Gilbert: An Improvisation, works quite explicitly to explore
or reconcile the ambitions he set for himself:

> i am a passing thing
> in which i am a subject—
> read my lines, be my mind.
> i am absolutely
> the I in the writing,
> the dead refuse to sing.

"Into the Into" is almost a somber presage of the next decade's
blocks or silences or refusals. When I emailed Elizabeth Alexander
about Gilbert, she said she'd never met him, but she knew his
work. She'd called him a few years before he died wanting to in-
clude him in an anthology: "He was quiet, said he'd been dealing
with chronic illness. Not friendly but not unfriendly. Said he had
new poems but never sent them." She ended the message with a
very earnest question: "Maybe he is the most original poet of his
generation? Possible."

By the early 1990s, Gilbert was a psychology professor at
Bristol Community College in Fall River, Massachusetts. What-
ever the difficulties—illness, doubt, discouragement—Gilbert's

poems remained in the world. In the remarkable title poem "Chris Gilbert: An Improvisation," someone so like Christopher Gilbert he calls himself Christopher Gilbert is in the hospital after one of the surgeries that, as we now know, will not ultimately save him:

> The scar the surgeon left as a signature
> on my belly's right side will say, "I am." I am
> I feel a gathering possibility passing from temporary
> articulation to articulation the way the horizon
> arises in the sun as a series of evident illuminations
> while the earth spins clockwise toward futurity.
> When the time comes I'll rise and say, "I am."
> I'll gather all my questions, step into their midst
> and say, "I am." I am I am.

The poem is an indication that, yes, Christopher Gilbert was beautifully striving "to be" all through his life. I imagine him fine-tuning, dismantling, and reassembling the book as if it was a self. The poems do not seem abandoned or forgotten or disregarded. They seem to anticipate the care of his family, friends and fans. We have the new work because of people like Fran Quinn, Ed Pavlic, Jeffrey Shotts, and Mark Doty. We have the new work because of the poet Mary Fell's skill and instincts in shaping it. The poetry of Christopher Gilbert seems to have anticipated the moment we would be here asking, "Who is Christopher Gilbert?" Even in his absence, he continues to insist "I am."

Terrance Hayes

Across the Mutual Landscape

Winner of the 1983 Walt Whitman Award

This book is dedicated
to my mother and father

This Bridge Across

A moment comes to me
and it's a lot like the dead
who get in the way sometimes
hanging around, with their ranks
growing bigger by the second
and the game of tag they play
claiming whoever happens by.
I try to put them off
but the space between us
is like a country growing closer
which has a language I know
more and more of me is
growing up inside of, and
the clincher is the nothing
for me to do inside here
except to face my dead
as the spirits they are,
find the parts of me in them—
call them back with my words.
Ancestor worship or prayer?
It's a kind of getting by—
an extension of living
beyond my self my people taught me,
and each moment is a boundary
I will throw this bridge across.

I. FIRE GOTTEN BRIGHTER

Resonance

In a back room
upstairs crouched over crystal
set, the dark headphones a cap
worn to finish the circuit.

Touching the quartz, a wave
would roll its clear tongue
against the windows, the dark
midwest faces came looking into—
spaces struck deep in the bone.

And I pulled the cat's whisker,
rolled the coil in hope,
from my hands a phoenix fluttered—
the lid of teenage body
a throbbing shell at sea.

Listening, I could hear
the whole Black house was music;
my brother playing Wes Montgomery downstairs
on the turntable, a lost double
octave rolling round through the air.

Pushing

Me and my brother would jump off the porch
mornings for a better view of the cars
that raced around the corner up Olds Ave.,
naming the make and year; this was '58
and his voice still young enough to wait for
how I'd say the names right to the air.
Cold mornings in Lansing we'd stop the mile
to school in the high-priced grocery nearly there
and the owner, maybe a decent White man
whose heavy dark hair and far Lebanese look
had caught too many kids at his candy,
would follow us down the aisles and say,
"I know what you boys is up to, big-eyed
and such, so you better be going your way—
buy something or else you got to leave."
We'd rattle the pennies we had and go
but coming home buy some nutchews to stay
and try his nerve again, because we didn't steal
but warmed ourselves till Ray would ask me why—
till, like big brothers will, one day I guessed,
"Some things you do because you want to.
Some things you do because you can't."
In what midwest warmth there was we'd laugh,
throw some snowballs high where the sun was
breaking up the clouds.

And, Yes, Those Spiritual Matters

Elegy for Robert Hayden

Whisper it,
"Oh Hayden,
he can do energy."

The words breaking in flower,
the breath on things
wearing bright new clothes.

The drums, bells, gods
in poemstate, speaking—
or hushin' each other.

The goofy dust
he threw in our tea materialized into
a story the class choked on.

Whisper it as he saw it—
intensely, the material part of being
is style.

Summons the Gabriel
half of him, the silent
leftover talk in your head.

Marking Time

for Freda Robertson

Jogging out in the morning
against the few high clouds the blue
sky is a memory like a sheer silk fabric
held so far back I can't see through it—
when I breathe the new air my body
is young all over, a smell reminds
how the two pear trees are white
again, their flowers ephemeral
as the words I recite to pass time
in repetitious wheezed breath—
squirrels, blue jays, downed trees for markers
to say how far I've gone, to be used
in their brief names to crowd my mind
with anything I can count on.
Today as I struggle against the wind
up the hill I watch a small butterfly
wavering with spread wings, and remember
dreaming of my sister who called
last night when I was sleeping, and how
twenty years ago she gave me
from the held darkness of her brown palms
a black butterfly with yellow specks.
What it was she said is immaterial,
there is the gesture though:
and watching a bird overhead fly
past the disk of sun, there is a flaring
shadow fanned down from above
that flickers like a rustled page

with a poem on it; it is that quick
flute darkness of a sister's voice
a brother will hear in his heart
when he's breathing deep enough.

Muriel Rukeyser as Energy

She knows the resonant dark
and she won't be bound.

She goes into.
A darkness has to touch,
and she wants to be exact.

She knows about the burning.
Her history is binary—
one of her hands is ash.

She's always being born.
She doesn't look away;
her sex is coming forward.

Ask her if there's laughter.
The frog in her head is jumping.
Myths arise where it sets.

She rides a flying horse.
It's red; she's stroking its neck.
She praises where it sweats

because the horse is available,
because it is required;
she loves its rascal mouth.

She wants to celebrate.
You know her reaching for words
and arranging them as fruit

knowing there is war,
and cities rising and falling, and
a river flowing with at least one shore.

She is the speed of darkness—
witness her mystery, not her gown.
As she tires, as she dies,

Aphrodite is getting smaller
but she's also burning hotter.
She is the dark one
and she won't be bound.

She

for Carolyn Grace

When she sits at the kitchen table
while she talks her hands seem to balance
in the air faithful at the level of
her words; she is careful what she says.
The morning sun through the window strikes
her skin, shows how the faint lines in her
palms will come to deepen like corduroy
cloth to fit the weather of her age.
Still a young woman, she has to work
the graveyard shift, sleeps what is left,
then wakes to get the kids to school.
It must be morning when she dreams.
Peering into her coffee's surface
she looks back from its depth, her hands
caught holding an implement, a fossil of
her life: Alabama born, feelings
huddled north, these steel cities this cold month,
her dark soul twisting into fingers
whose motion at this brown angle
is the slow fall flight of leaves through time.
And she rises with the gesture, and
the oil in her hands is necessity's
sweat: each hand on the tabletop
a work cloth rubbing the other fine
wooden one.

Time with Stevie Wonder in It

Winter, the empty air, outside
cold shaking its rigid tongue
announcing itself like something stone,
spit out, which is still a story
and a voice to be embraced.
Januaried movements but I hear a tune
carries me home to Lansing.

Always waiting for signs of thaw,
dark nomads getting covered by snow,
our parents would group in the long night—
tune frequencies to the Black stations
blasting out of Memphis, Nashville,
still playing what was played down south—
Ray Charles, Charles Brown, Ruth Brown, Muddy and Wolf.

The tribal families driven north
to neighborhoods stacked like boxes—
to work the auto plants was progress,
to pour steel would buy a car
to drive hope further on down the road.
How could you touch, hear
or be alive; how could anybody

wearing our habits, quiet Protestant
heads aimed up to some future?
This was our rule following—
buy at J.C. Penney and Woolworth's,
work at Diamond Reo, Oldsmobile, Fisher Body.
On Fridays drink, dance, and try to forget
the perverse comfort of huddling in

what was done to survive (the buffering,
the forgetting). How could we not
"turn the head/pretend not to see?"
This is what we saw: hope screwed
to steel flesh, this was machine city
and the wind through it—neutral
to an extent, private, and above all

perfectly European language
in which we could not touch, hear
or be alive. How could anybody
be singing "Fingertips?" Little Stevie
Wonder on my crystal, 1963.
Blind boy comes to go to school,
the air waves politely segregated.

            ·‿

If this were just a poem
there would be a timelessness—
the punchclock midwest would go on
ticking, the intervals between ticks
metaphor for the gap in our lives
and in that language which would not
carry itself beyond indifferent

consequences. The beauty of the word,
though, is the difference between language
and the telling made through use.
Dance Motown on his lip, he lays
these radio tracks across the synapse
of snow. The crystals show
a future happening with you in it.

Fire Gotten Brighter

Remember that memory.
In this dimness when the sounds I make
are foreign, my home is not my own
when I think of another winter
and the distant whiteness of its walls—
when even the sun seems set
outside the world. In this dimness
the edge of things removed
to thought the numb call touch,
remember that memory—
the young black self
the whole black body painted hot
by the fresh orange scene in the basement
of our old house when I was nine.
When it was my turn
to keep the fire going while my family slept—
my father off divorced somewhere, my older brother resting
after work, and what shadows hovered at the fringe of light
spilt from the furnace's mouth—
I struck my shovel in the flame,
had its intensity
its heat travel through a vein in the handle
to a part of my head.
The coals gotten smaller, brighter.
Out of that fire, my frightened shoveling in the night
now a framed power, that young effort
made a little orange scene
kept the whole world excited—
gathered near its center.

In this dimness where I can't tell
if my longing is my own, it is gotten winter.
Above me I watch a jet
that be's perfectly still, yet gets so distant,
goes so pointless. I could take a plane,
fly from here to somewhere small
till I'm ashes of myself—
but everything burns repeatedly
or keeps burning. Remember that memory.
I am dark with effort, back at my mother's house
someone's thinking of me, an old and smothered flame
gets waked, and it warms the gap
between image and real light.

·~ II. THE MOMENT GETTING SO

Now

I park the car because I'm happy,
because if everyone parked we'd have a street party,
because the moon is full—
it is orange, the sky is closer
and it would be wrong to drive into it.
This is the first day of summer—
everyone is hanging out,
women walk by in their bodies so mellow
I feel I'm near a friend's house

The small white flakes of the headlights
sweat for a second on the storefronts.
In the windows, darkened afterhours,
a reflection stares back
looking more like me than me.
I reach to touch
and the reflection touches me.
Everything is perfect—
even my skin fits.

Hanging out,
the taillights of the turning cars
are fires, going out—
are the spaces of roses flowered
deeper in themselves. I close my eyes
and am flowered deeper in myself.
Further up the street a walking figure
I can't make out, a face
behind a bag of groceries, free arm swinging
in the air the wave of a deep red
fluid shifting to and fro.

At the vegetarian restaurant
I see it's Michael the Conga Drummer—
been looking for him 2 months.
He asks me, "What's happening."
I love his fingers.
When we shake hands I mix his grip
with the curve of my father's
toting cantelope in the house from the market.
We are two griots at an intersection.
I answer him in parable:
the orange that I've been carrying
is some luminous memory, bursting,
bigger than my hand can hold,
so I hand him half.

Exactly Passing Through (Horn Player)

The need we have to deny the way things have to be
more than themselves. Otherwise, like the air moving
from room to room, things outgrow the terms we have
to contain them in. Otherwise we would feel our bodies
as abandoned places and our deep caresses as hollow rubs.
Yet right now I hear the chive stretching in its planter
on the windowsill, and I will go outside to see its purple
baby blossoms falling and the ideal blue air dissolving
into the skyline, into the hard blue uniform of the cop,
or the wild eyes of the lost boy, and I won't suffer.

The horn player on the corner up ahead understands
as though he has a seventh sense where everything matters:
the stalled red car, the girl learning to ride her bike
one-handed against the traffic down the street,
the Irish Setter howling, and that siren slowly pulsing.
The tune he is playing is hassled but a perfect line
of speech (which doesn't mean that you can hear it—yet).
This corner is part of his flesh, new cells he connects
into one piece. And what he is he is as by-product
in what he plays, the incidental seed which gathers
the nearby rain which happens to swell in August. Music.

Such a swelling so as I get closer the terms I use
to assert us, imperfect though they are, are gestures
toward a future perfect body. Meaning there is a connection
between what I say and the way we will be in the world.
Perfect as though I am saying, *Blessed Other Come Closer,*
as a wholly new animal awakes shedding what it knows
to simply become another presence among things, disclosed
and passing through first one surface and then another.

Awaking as, Oh God, being in this scene together
our attention is blue-insistent and forward-looking,
a kind of sky which has gained a way of being inside
its wholeness—not ideal nor abstract but exactly
what is happening.

Semiotic Function

Over the course of the month
her belly expands; 5 pounds of water
pressures itself against me
when I pull her near and am drawn
towards her.

Our bodies laying together,
two objects in the room
reaching for that moment when
they fuse again, like everything
in motion in itself. Like our words
rushing forward to connect so deep
who can say where they come from.

"Do you really want to?"
she says. "Men are afraid of women
on the rag. Why be nice
to hide how you feel."

Does it matter that I want to?
What I do I don't know
more than that single act
when I hug the flesh
of her stomach, or hang onto
the swell of her hip.
There are questions I can't answer

as: "when the tide comes in
what wild fear it might hide
is reason enough
where motion is concerned?"

Kite-Flying

June at Truro Beach the joyous bathers,
specks of jewel fallen along the sand.
Walking near them there is this polarity—
their lives the way stars hold to the sky.
The morning sun chuckles across wave-tops
weightless as warm breath; we watch it float
like holy stone skipping toward Gennesaret.
Against the wind the kite quibbles and bobs
in our hands mad as any tethered bird—
it thinks it is a gull and wants to be with them.
And we are molecules of air, heated up,
spread in this big lab on the beach to launch it.

Every dream is a moment of freedom
and for the while when the kite goes up,
chest bowed forward, our thoughts race ahead
like anything light enough to fly; so crazy
holding the line, my one arm raised ready to flap
and wing, forgetting the kite has limits, and we
will suffer the air between two beached stones.
But what does the impulse know when it rises
up the nerve to the head? That it is—
whether body or thought is needless conclusion.
Today the gray haddock are utterly silver.
A naked girl rides by on a dripping horse.
Every line of words we say is radiant floss
let go.

The Surviving

I wake in dream in the middle of night
and know without looking a frost has come
and is killing the delicate garden plants.
Without looking I walk to the backyard—
feel the cool leaves of the squash gone limp.
As they press themselves against my flesh
they are the tears on the face of a survivor
who finds his village gone. Ice is forming
in their veins, many leaves will droop tomorrow
black and rubbery. Now they lean toward me
expecting sunlight or a warm breeze—
and I look back to the house and wish
my friend would flick the lights, press her face
against the glass to signal me back.
While now she may be calling my name but
calling from deep inside her separate dream,
as the garden divides: one for her head, its twin
in mine. The world and I detach from each other,
the tactile garden forms become ugly
discoveries like those muffled agonies
that rise unfocused from the television news—
the nuclear dust amassing in the 1980s,
the faraway battles in the Mid-East,
the anonymous burned skin in a city slum.
Without some grace the plant is a self—
these squash hover here like Kollwitz' survivors—
figures battered so far their substance sinks inward.
And the spirit found outside its housing? It breaks.
It becomes the detail that is forgotten,
the lone figure walking his own road, dispirited
and not fated to have at hand a way back.

It's all so mythic a representation:
the figure aimlessly wandering might be the mind
and what is being looked for is some act
bad enough to express it, to improvise,
to say it is, to see itself start from scratch
while the crazy path of history might be dying.
But this is living, and the belief in being in
the world of symbols is nothing I can relate to now.
A form of sufficiency is what we live for.
I startle. Across the field heavy diesels clang
rumbling down the highway, their headlights jarring.
Come morning winds we will breathe their grit.
Without thinking I pick the ready squash,
press these dense dark bodies against my chest,
carry them back to the house like babies.
Because these losses I know we will wake.

Touching

Light is a distant world
though at 5 a.m. in the bedroom
window where the spider plant hovers
shining, there is a silken presence
where it traces, leaves a constellation.
I roll over and the room moves
a little closer, it is light-
like when Karen sleeps beside me
turned away but warm rubbing back
and I curve myself like hers
to hold her body for seeing
whatever is far in her.
Now I'm almost dreaming.
Words run transparent from my mouth
and almost find the edge of things.
Across the street in the park
a big hawk sails, gently flapping,
its outspread arms hugging the air
just as the sun kisses upward
to find its way through the sky.
Back here off the edge of the bed
my fingers, blind at both ends,
dangle in a void like starlight
travelled so far its source burned out.
Now a light goes off in my head as
I hold this hand that seems so far away.
I think of the monster fullback
in high school, after running over me
he dropped the ball to see was I hurt.
Where is he now, or the woman
who put the message in the bottle

I found splashing in the fouled waters
off Point Pelee. What was on her mind
writing, *kindness anywhere is still kindness,*
I'm in Cleveland, cold, alone—
wherever you are you hold this part of me.
I roll over in the glow
where sunrise goes across the bed,
knowing our age thinks light is wavelike
bundles spreading outward like ships
floating home in measured gaps toward each shore.
So part of the world waits distant.
For all I know as a man it might happen
like kelp bits drifting to no shore.
Still if there's a moment somewhere
equal to this light filling my skin,
then there is a constant I can count on
and I'll go forth and live with that.

Listening to Monk's *Mysterioso*
I Remember Braiding My Sisters' Hair

What it's all about is being
just beyond a man's grasp,
which is a kind of consciousness
you can own, to get to
be at a moment's center
and let it keep on happening
knowing you don't own it—

which is moving yourself close to, being
particular to that place. Like my two sisters
taking turns braiding each others' hair—
hair growing against their weaving, they formed
a flow their hurt and grace could mean
as each took turns pulling the comb through
the other's knots and their little Vaseline.

A knowing which makes the world
a continuity. As in your core
something calls to you
at a distance which does not matter.
As in the world you will see yourself
listening to follow like water
following its wave to shore.

To arrive in your life you must
embrace this letting, letting
which is a match for the stream
through flowering field and the tall trees
wandered into and the river wearing beads
just ahead which you go into
further on because you can.

This going so is something else—the way
it flows into always something deeper and
over your head, a kid with "why" questions.
Your answer is a moment struggling to be
more than itself, your straining for air
to have the chance to breathe it free.
It's alive you've come to,

this coming into newness, this dis-
continuous mind in you looking up, finding
an otherness which trusts what you'll become—
for me, my sisters once offering,
"You want to learn to braid my hair."
If we are blessed in this world
it is in feeling *this*—

i.e., there are circumstances
and you are asked to be
their member. Not owning but owning in—
a participation, like Monk's implied words
reaching for their sentence: "If you can
get to it. . . ."

III. HORIZONTAL COSMOLOGY

Horizontal Cosmology

1. *The Backyard*

Suddenly this voice is calling
when I go to the backyard.
The garden leaves cut the wind to singing
and their bodies, the perfect green
instruments for what they do.

The tree next door whose leaves
are phrases falling
where the wind is blowing,
the arpeggio of the Charlie Parker tune—
and impossible flight of notes.
And I'm humming to myself.

I will work the day out here, singing.
It makes me a gift with myself.
Something to make the yard bigger.
My hands fall at my sides, octaves apart.
How far? Clear enough for my friends
who look for me to feel between them.

2. *The Moment Getting So*

October, and the wind getting so
things cover themselves from it or else
become it, become bare and blue,
then a wide bodiless trembling. I'm
watching the backyard squirrels find food,
truck their catch to hide in holes.
I pick the last tomatoes mid-fall,
their stalks turned yellow-tinged and dry.
Stakes tie their stems to hold them up.
The red outlines of the fruit shrivel
and shrink. Growing inward from the wind
they become the zero promise of air,
leaning toward the shape of slience.
In August they weighed in my hands like fire.
Today it grows so cool by evening
I forget what I've come outside for,
I grow nostalgic for sweating.
The sun goes behind the house next door
by six; when I stretch on tiptoe
it shines on the front part of my neck;
high on my toes I shift and swallow,
wishing my body could be a husk,
could hold the sun's ripe flower forever.
As for what these plants are doing, this
exact moment in the cold, they stand for
the urge to be inside or else
their thoughts, dark and amazingly flush
with the bottomless landscape.

3. *Fetish*

The wind comes down and terrifies so,
bringing back the holes in my clothes.
I'd lost them in the painless summer
air that fit like laughter in a round room.
I would rather the wind was a thing—
a professional I could close the door to.
I would rather the wind could be paid up—
an object in the supermarket's aisle
walked by and it demanding no more
than a TV show fixed on my glasses.
It's cold, I tell myself to buy something—
I wonder if my charge accounts are safe,
if the lamp still works and the car has gas.
I would rather the wind didn't howl
like fears through the cracks in the walls.
I open and close the refrigerator.
Suddenly the phone rings. I turn my back,
scared the voice down it might be a flame.
Scared I am an object the voice would pray to.

4. *Saxophone*

My bell is Charlie Parker's
hatband. So few of you who
come to touch me understand
my feeling,
only this black voice.
I am a temple and he comes
to speak through me. I am the dream
lip because
I say what you're afraid of
facing, *Living is intense.*

I am bad from note to note
like god's nostril, I connect
living to what lies ahead
by breath.
You want to know how to feel
in this world, the technology
bigger than the ear? Listen,
I can't tell you what to hear.
I have no message waiting
for you: you must be-
hold enough to play.

5. *Speaking Things*

In the house at night,
the body in shallow sleep
wants to remember something, but
remember as though it was
but is not now a consequence:
the way a scene is centered in the mind
while you are out there in it.
In the house a wet sax tune
drones over a funk fabric,
dark and silksyllable bursting open
and then the taste of rhythm.
The tune passes by. No one cares
enough to open himself to it.

Deeper in the dream the body wakes,
goes through the house breathing the song.
What a deep connection.
The man wakes and isn't the same. Listening
all day long marking his words
respectfully for the music he says is
in his house. His speech falls on things:
bread, beer, beef, and—salt peanuts—
not unlike those notes the horn would say.

6. *The Facts*

Looking down the empty Mason jars
in the cupboard, I forget myself.
I forget my name and its belongings.
I forget my plastic ID card
for the "Y," my Exxon credit card
and the square feeling it leaves in my hand.
I forget passing thirty and feeling nothing—
but dreaming blue tears that night all the same.
I forget wanting money, no, wanting
to be like the men who have money,
who piss against the wall of good fortune.
I forget wanting the honest work
that poor people do, the necessary
work a man will do despite his fortunes,
the unsour laboring for the next life's wealth.
I forget the violinist 10 years ago
playing scales, narrowing her long attention
almost Buddha-like to one fluid note.
I forget the days in the auto plant
doing seventy bodies per minute—
the tools continuous in one loud scream,
the pinch, punch, press, and pounding of steel—
a gray space inside myself driven
like a car to the next stop down the line.
I forget all the textbook recipes
and all the facts I never lived in school.
I forget the facts I lived: the wet kiss
in the heart of all events drying out.
I forget Worcester, Mass.; Oakland;

Lansing, Michigan; and Birmingham;
their industrial dream frozen in mid-air,
a black wind crying over this lost scene,
and my white words unable to call it in.
I forget Birmingham again and being born
in that foundry town, feeling 1950s
no-english baby except to act, "fuck you,"
fat new-born feet remembering an old dance,
kicking at the balls of the steelman's statue
that hovered over town like a speechless god.
I forget further back the rocking in water;
the water always becoming 2 kinds—
the mother water and the nightmare water
where a man will drift from home in chains.
I forget the magic gourd that fit my hands,
its shake my feeling of having a heart.
My face is a mask. Everyone wears it.
When I take if off there's another face.
I turn around to you, you this moment
I have come to empty-handed and not myself.

I am between things—what's going on?
I'm stuck. You stare with expectation.
You want a sacrifice. You take my breath.
My arm drifts off to light the stove.
The walls heave and blacken with body salt.
The cupboards fireball toward some purpose.
You want my green tomatoes stored to ripen?
Why you gaze outward, brother?
You look off like a wanderer. You mad.

You the air and there's nothing set to fill.
You making a stew. You demand something read.
I put a record on. One saxophone
and the room remembers, Bird lives!
This is my body, the horn-words say.
Bird's forwards music a feeling which is:

> *Start with another man's line.*
> *Stamp it with your point of view.*
> *Space is terms; meaning is glue,*
> *and each step you take is time.*
> *You write your self with what you do—*
> *dazzling being the world's mind.*

You stop the record, you demand something read.
It's *your* story you say, fuck Bird, the way
Bird would have put it nicely through his sax.
Listen, Chris, the mask is artifact.
There's no substitute to live for you.
Life is here; for you to be it live
without a charm to cleanse its chances.
There's no getting past its confrontations.
There just ain't. You stand atop tradition
practicing whatever is your music, lip torn
on false starts, out of breath and no one else
to play your part, your million facts—
but when your number's flashed you play.

Suppose I were to say:
Simmer soul from African water

4 centuries on disintegrating train,
no stops. No mule no 40 acres.
Remove the umbilical tongue.
Add salt to wounds repetitively.
Let stand in cold.
Remove the perfect laughing.
Look out for small movements.
Cover and boil.
Remove vestiges of celestial knowledge.
Omit a dream opened out on the world.
Forget the oblique signifying.
Sprinkle maleficence and malfeasance.
When gall arises, keep bottled. 32 years.
Remove the bits of tenderness.
Bring yourself from nothingness.

＿

Suppose I were to say:

I leave myself for the future of the spinach seed flying away in the sudden breeze. A breeze goes all the way in the contours of things.

I have decided to land someday when you know me better. Right inside your ear. I'll grow inward there. The dark questions inside you will align themselves along me and feel my boundaries as intimate as answers.

I leave myself with the speechlessness of the poor woman widowed from her old neighborhood by the shining buildings and the mayor's new plans.

I have decided to shake the backyard pear tree and to throw its hard young fruit. If there is any timing they'll shatter glass and burst in justice in a litany of flame.

I leave myself and become the black body in a southern town. I am a citizen so I have this hope. One of my arms moves north to Chicago and sings the blues. One of my arms moves west to Texas and sings the blues.

I have decided to be the long black language that reaches all the way back. When I get there I keep on reaching. I write this off as jazz. Part of me is laughing at my situation. That part is the old griot walking the world, learning the zen of laughter.

I leave myself for the many versions of light as the sun comes across the rippled spit of the Atlantic.

I have decided to be the boat's prow while you're the pier. I'm tied to you. When the tide comes in I rock forward and kiss the wet black splinter on your forehead just above the water's level. There is sweat in both our mouths. You change into Yeats's glimmering girl. Your tongue speaks sunlight rising up your throat.

I have decided my joy is the rising surface of rain water in a bucket during a midwest storm. Suddenly the sky is Canadian cold clear. I give off speckles of light and am the dark patina that gathers it. I'll set myself beside the trail where you walk by. I wish you luck, you this world's blue thirst. You might be Malcolm X with one of Roethke's roses in your vest. You know the arithmetic of a double thirst. It's the same old loneliness that made Coltrane disappear. This time I'll be of use.

I have decided to be background vocal in a 60s Motown song. A grown-up adolescent love song I can leave myself in my hips to. Maybe the Temptations singing. Get ready.

I have decided to become one of Mary Driscoll's kids if she'll have me—one semester. She'll read Vallejo, and I'll be Lorca listening. Her furious Celt films are in the cupboard at her house. She keeps a projector handy. It's pure voodoo when her thing's cranked up.

I have decided to be American again, sitting naked at night on a rock in the low waters of West River, Brattleboro, 1981. Knowing poetry alone won't save us from the Russian nukes or the big Yankee Nuke and James Watt for that matter, drinking lite beer and eating corn buttered from absurdly poisoned cows. When a small fish veers too close I see its nightmare flash in its one glowing eye. It darts away renouncing our kind, and I want to be with it. Choose a far-off object and cast my spirit to it. American willing too much and too little, I cannot shed myself. I can't feel my spirit as it already swims among these circumstances till I swim my seasons of fault and loss, till I swim the recesses of the people and things I love and am connected to.

I have decided to be myself again. Thank you fahlet'n me be myself again. Thank you fahlet'n me be myself again. Thank you   fahlet'n me   be myself   again.

.‿

Suppose I were to say:
I know my birth because I pronounce myself transformed.
I know my age 'cause any age will do. Age is trite because each year
    the wars go on and on, continuous and eternal.
I know my country because while I travel I meet the cowboys
    who own it.
    We are all of one tongue, we say every word but *friend*.
    This is their custom, this absent speech.
I know not what is lost, but I know grief is not.
I know my pride because I don't look back.
I know my shame because across the world there are people dying
    I pretend I don't know. This is that shame of looking in a
    mirror at a face pretending it knows nothing of the dying even
    as its honesty is killed.

I know my rage because I burn. Mortal and sacrificial, I become
 united with what is lost. Now I know that I am real.
I know my language as these words I have to say. Saying, *this*, is
 not an excuse for this.
I know my self speaking my voice. When it is wholly exact it mat-
 ters, and I am proof the things it will come to touch talk back.
I know this is a journey, and I have gone this far. I make use of
 where I am.

Suppose I were to say:
The self grows, the self goes forward,
the self goes forward out of its presentness,
a batch of moments where what is being is
the meeting in each moment, the breath where it is.

Age 5, near drowning in the Red Cedar; the excited
boy holding on to the water which rocked, brown-black
and summer warm; lungs unable to fill with air, wanting
then to swallow the whole of water; thrashing for some
last breath while listening to the river in his head;
the absolute music of the water too holy to stand
apart from; yes, to go fully forward is to lose the self;
yes, I wanted to merge with the water music, be fluid in it
to make the world be dream again, whole and on-coming.
For a flash this moment mattered, not: the shore; the others
ahead swimming, their black inner-tubes standing out atop
the surface; the dry midwest republican morals half-accepted
like the insufferable air—till I gave myself over to a wave
and came up convinced of swimming in the waters
on the shore.

You find the self at these moments:
the collection of possible completions and real dreams
converging like streams into one mellifluous river
rushing forward toward itself.

The live moment, a wave
comes and I am one with water,
and when I stand outside the moment
thinking my loss, the self comes forward—
like fishermen dropping anchor
this mark, this reference against chaos.
A moment lost wandering
where no one was waiting to hear
has come home to papa.
Its flesh full like jars
on a shelf—YES, LORD, YES
I'VE FOUND THE STEWED TOMATOES.
While the chili is cooking
I am writing something—
for now, I've decided
let this writing be my name.
When the recipe is done
(if it's good, if it's me)
I'll be the person eating.
And the self grows,
the self grows forward,
the self grows forward
out of its reference.

IV. BEGINNING BY EXAMPLE

(from the Willie poems)

Beginning by Example

He is walking across the lawn
in the picture framed through your window,
a blob about to spill through the glass
between you. Like there is no lock—
just the wind between his body
and what he will be in the world.
Just your life which he must break in.
Secretly you move the glass.
Though it is a mirror, you wonder
are there more of him out there.
A chant against the weather,
your question is killing the risk.
Quickly, you call him *Willie*
and summon him with a name counted on
like Adam scared out of the coming dark
put his young mind against the view,
naming things to fit his image.

Today the man outside your words
looks through his own frame. What he sees
you can't see. You're blind to the soul.
You think he's strange, wild, frail.
But he is walking the world's gland,
pure language on his shoulders.
When will you recognize the signs?—
his body fogging the glass with its breath
till everything you see is colored
by his words. They mean the atmosphere
to you: the bruise-blue street shining

with rain, the live whine of the traffic
out there with a lone jive-man dancing
in it, the masses of specific items
all feeling, like nothing in your world.

Blue

Everyone is gone. Everyone.
At a gutted store building
in his old neighborhood
Willie idles, kicking the rubbish.
By chance the odd pieces gather
into a stick figure—a boy.
Willie adds bits of cloth
and an old mop head for hair,
but he finds no object to be
a word to coax his boy to talk.
The face is a cracked white plate.
Willie throws it to the road
hoping a tire explodes.
The image exists when it confirms
our sense of being. Willie feels blue
like the sky, so close so far away.
When he opens his mouth
there is no sound but a window.
He opens it wide to show more air.

Beginning by Destruction

Today I stumble over something
resembling a dead person.
I look down at the body—
a loose skin holding it in.
I lift an arm from the ground.
The whole thing stinks. I start to go
but feel there's something left to do.
How many years have gone
with me sad, wishing him alive.
He is a totemic thing—
I stare the reflection in his eyes.

You touch the body, the parts
gathered by a suit of clothes.
You punch it, push your knife in
because now it is your turn.
You think about the pieces like they were
clues, existing for your ends.
As you fascinate yourself
with what it's like being dead, disembodied,
feel the fear you have of living,
as you kill the pure event. Realize:
Death is an absolute real event.

Willie wakes feeling the wound you've made
believing him a dead matter.
Through his life the space that was
is sharp and filled now with presence—
even if that part of him is flawed.
Knowing the NOT of death emphasizes
life's YES. The glow of his phrasing

as he finds a way to forgive
your being. As he struggles to not
be shaped by the wounds you bring
but to make something with those wounds.

Beginning by Value

What about his feelings—
a woman might understand them
because she doesn't let go
without bearing things inside.
The bearing like a mother will
staring into the womb in her,
then further into her child.
Bearing the way an atmosphere
is the message felt in-between
two bodies, is the language
both bodies share in common—
a part of each said in the other.
So Willie's birth is like your own,
but not till now did you much care
if his feelings were your own.
Recognize he is the knowledge
which is not in your heart.
He feels the cold of distance.
Something in you used to leave him
there to *bear it like a man*.
It is wrong to have to feel
that cold, and you know it.

Like

Here's another version of him:
At dawn outside what was once
Reo Truck in Lansing, he wants
spare change for coffee,
the time of day or directions,
then asks me for his name.
I call him *Willie*. He hunches
down in his coat, a root
scared of being left exposed.

He must have come from somewhere
to stand outside these buildings
moaning in his folded hands,
trying to maybe find himself
by conjuring to remember better,
maybe to find the steady job
hoping trucks are in demand—
a busy plant with its white
tick of machinery rhyming.

Overhead the powerlines limp
in their black skins, wanting
to ground their distance.
Spent, there's no potential
need to carry their hum to.
They exist to remind Willie of
the empty ledger lines he's walked
measuring the miles but always
at their end. Whether this is
his city or not, he's done arrived.
And he moans. From the inside.

We look and glimpse a large bird
whose name I don't know
fluttering above the factory roof.
Against the morning sun it becomes
suddenly immense and wonderful—
because the sky measures little.
Willie, standing in the bird's shadow,
simply is—a man never so alive.
More real because there was never
none of his deliberate self
inside those walls to compare him to.

The Directions

Down the street the ground is feeling so
the dancer hotfoots, lifting his leg
right enough that the floor sparks,
bursts in flame to jump the gap
between himself and its dark nerve
(therefore wherever he moves
he gets a sense of where he stands).
The sky has always wanted something
to belong to it. Its backward gravity
pulls the dancer's shape, and he flies
upward in himself airy in the mind.

Any haint treading a tightwire
looks for a window to climb through—
motion is the dancer's solution
to every space. Willie struts and
the world is a woman he wants
to arouse but not all the way
give himself to. His afterthought:
to spend himself despite himself.
Someone left a damn blue light burning
in his brain. He moves with it
and his future comes aglow.
Don't want things; want the spirit of them.
Recognize faith is an horizon.
Wherever you move you go toward home.

Any Good Throat

July, on the basketball court,
Willie's face is far and wooden
totem, his eyes melted pools of ice
shimmering in the high stone sun—
the sockets are darkness rotting inside.
Fifteen and can't get a summer job—
because of this the traffic jams,
the high school windows cloud with phlegm.
All day long the poison of waiting
for the sharp need in his gut to be
more than its meaning in your mind,
for the name in his blood to ring
louder than this killing in his heart,
staring all day out the same caged grin
because it doesn't matter,
because this tarred-over earth
burned and raped and cheated of growth
where his friends come root like acorns
fallen from some wound up tree
is more mother than any gray voice
in the city he might hear.

So we give him a ball
and he slams the thing luminously,
so the rim swallows its circle and cries.

A music I've heard these evenings
draws me out, whoever I am,
past the sweet sweatdown in the late sun
silence up to my knees where I bend

in the backyard working up burdock roots'
grip tapped down a good half-foot,
emerges in the saline welling in my mouth
and the work-song rhythm hummed in my hands
pulling the hoe back and forth and back,
working in an honest groove, and what
with the blunder some god done made
putting me here in the world to choose
what thing is weed and what is food
makes me want to say, *Amen*
and ripen in my *Willie*-night and sing.

·⌣

In the evening indigo off the road
near the reservoir a waterfall
trickles, only waist-wide, winding down
to dam behind then spill around dead sticks
in slow gurgle toward water basin
heavy and warm after a humid week.
Along the way there are hesitations
where layers of rock rise up awkward like
molars blocking thought in mid-sentence—
their volume a venturi for a moment
that, like any good throat, intensifies things,
then thrusts the waters forward in song.

Charge

Gimme the ball, Willie is saying
throughout this 2-on-2 pick-up game.
Winners are the ones who play, being
at the sidelines is ridiculous.
So what happens here is a history
won not by the measure of points,
but by simply getting into it.
Willie plays like it could all be gone
at once, like his being is at stake.
Gimme the ball, he cusses.
Gwen Brooks's player from the streets.
The game is wherever there's a chance.
It is nothing easy he's after,
but the rapture gained with presence.
His catalogue of moves represents
his life. Recognize its stance.
So alive to be the steps
in whose mind the symbol forms,
miraculous to be the feeling
which threads these steps to dance.
The other side is very serious—
they want to play him 2-on-1.
Messrs. Death and Uniformity.
He's got a move to make them smile.
Gimme the ball, Willie says again
and again, *Gimme the goddamn ball.*

Edges

In the drink light of disco, a limb
shines out of shadow, bends deftly out of brown wooded
stillness, becomes the body moving,
becomes a leg's walk homeward tracing the intuitive,
drumming the stretched skin of world.

With the feets' scratched step, etched
against whatever place
Willie remembers (the order in
steps a kind of creation), Willie
represents
and becomes his own author
reading his bruised pattern through time.

     ·ᴗ

Way back in '29 Lashley seemed to grasp
the bottomless store of memory, its edges
spread equally throughout the mind
swelling outward in the form of things—
in the eye mapping, in the tactile woo
of hand aligned with goal, in the right and left
ball, and the unfolding of vagina, in the thought:
the woman in the red dress reminds me of a friend, and in
the heart, a chart of all the person knows.

And what of the rat brain crying out in his lab,
    metaphoric squeaks
lost in the white noise of his consciousness?

     ·ᴗ

Beyond the frame of bar-room window
the billboards suggest food, and
with the oblique punch of hunger
bringing back his old body, an emotional
and political complex—
those near desecrated buildings pimped up
on Lansing's west side—
Black men leaning without work,
the straight dark edge of Willie's knife.

Our music is lost
till just a score remains—
this cold sequence,
tall empty barlines waving—
good-bye word magic, good-bye big ear.

     ·⌣

The right thinking
               doesn't want money.
doesn't declare war, doesn't
cry *wolf, weed, wino, willie,*
whore, honkey, or get half-involved,
but simply recognizes
the flower, the face, the edge
that is things.

Shapes hallucinate in the dim disco painting—
watery pattern of light splashed on rim of glass,
gravity's red lines spark on retina
and this bass boomed floor moans—
its being wholly stating itself.

Later, in a museum, the figure is Calder's *Big Red*.
All its nameless transcendent lines—
where the masses and red and wire extend—
lifts itself off the white background,
lifts itself so I have to wonder—
"Is it rooster, or rose, or
just reality testing?"
A luminous thing like *Willie*
who be's.

　　　　·〉

This matter, this commitment of
poem pieces said in their fit place, gathers in this form:
　　　Willie, a black man, yes,
a man, where his age hates the figurative,
kills the DOO-WOP, DOO-WOP plea of a body
poised always at edge, saying *this*,
against the ordinary.

Willie, always at his deathknell—
the raggedy end of his time
　　　and time, and
and time, so words flicker, jag
at the chaos precarious at the tip of my tongue.
His dance is what I know of him—
the leap to the crazy lip of fate,
his high-stepping
where the last light gathers, that line of
contrasts where the physical ends—
a figure toying with falling beyond it all,
the anxious exclamations falling from my mouth.

V. IN THE MUTUAL LANDSCAPE

The Clearing

Sitting at an intersection in the city
with what seems like 20,000 things to handle
and the traffic on the way to work is the first
which, like the other half-awake dreamers, I do
not because I choose but just to not waste time
which is never enough what with the rush hour snag
between here and the spot ahead where the traffic clears.
And there's a kind of loss, an inattention,
a meaning *less* because driving from here to that space
is just driving while I need to find a way to be—
a trust to go the distance between the absent
and how, say, the abstract buildings looming ahead
become concrete because I've gotten nearer—
a way I can be born congruent with my situation
and not be ignorant of my hand on the wheel
or the car's wheezing soot on the surface of my facts.

Each thing is itself. But this doesn't describe the future—
it stands ahead of me like a Latin sentence
whose verb I haven't come to, and this doesn't come close to
restricting the black cat poised by the curb, teasing the cars
between which he'll be an atmospheric abstraction which struts.
On one hand he stays on the side of the windshields
marked *other*. But his presence is the common bead of sweat
which bubbles on the drivers' skins. Everything near this corner
is his nature; so he's Spinoza's God, numinous
through the things around him and the traffic jam he makes.
But nobody promised eternity would bring an end
to the headache of stop-and-go driving. Maybe welcome it
as a reality and complete the integrity of it.
Ah shoot! I say to myself at this point, laughing

in the landscape, because there is this city street
and I am in it thinking there's nothing to rush on to
except the black cat and the clearing up ahead
and the steady way this moment is a road spreading
outward between two presences connected to itself.
I can't hardly wait till I get there.

Glimpses

Up the hillside beyond the road's
dirt edge the evening comes and the harvest
air holds the sun's warmth in a last burning
breath hanging overhead a fever to the sky.
Valley drifts towards the end of blue,
my dogs lose their selves with skunk stink,
wag their lives on squirrels' fat tracks.
A couple in the east walking Vermont in a spell,
finding a circling road which they pursue
forward as though they might be late. Moon
clears a tree blocking out horizon,
rose red swollen outside its distance.

Suddenly, as if some hold had broken,
the leaves fall one and then another
from that maple, like fires flickering downward
and, the moon sighs bigger than its mouth.
Hearing an animal's proud body ease
in the grass, I turn to my friend
whose face floats below a layer of sweat—
a light clay pot where juice flows over.
Her eyes reflect the wave of wind
through a field of hazel grain, and me
the beaming farmer knowing it is time.

Pitch

Another night the ballad sleeps.
Against the chaos of nightclub
the dim lights show a man at the bar,
his fingers scattered in private themes
unconnected but for the random
yearning wasted through his hands
as he reaching spills over his drink.
The air smoked, brown heads poke
in and out of this gray haze.
Numb bodies crowded, fun lovers
sleep-walking, finger-popping, light
jitterbugging arhythmic dance.
This is how it must have been
at those uptown clubs between sets.
No music but the polite talk,
the frozen hiss of background,
foreboding but so far away.
But then this other part—
the sudden breeze worth waiting for
when an owl will come, sweeping
across piano around midnight.
Its high-spread wings, the wild god-eye
plunging to perch on wood, then
pluck the soft dark movements below.
Now the figure of the man
is tapping the ballad out, and
how the dancers will awaken to
step the sequence of his hands.

.~

March, 1978, and the artist is
at her workbench looking down,
a cleared-away portion
of the kitchen table
pulled near the window facing east
where the sky comes in: oranges,
apples, and the one avocado
throw a heap of shadow
getting long ripening there.

This morning she can't work—
the music from the other room,
or was it the startled birds outside
that lift from the tree high up
where they seem to cry
in a brief shivering pattern?

Standing in the window she is
a house plant; her hands hanging
at her sides don't open though.
Today it will snow. In the east
a bus is bombed in Herzliya.
In the Atlantic, Canadian sealers
are breaking ice towards an island
and the waiting baby seals.

Back at her workbench she stares.
The shadow her form projects
taps its pen until the aching stops.
And then her hands open up

to rearrange the fruit, because
the music the morning asked for
has simply come to be like this.

⌐

A girl startles up from dream—
the boyfriend killed by the cops
had come home. An American hero
with tags and ribbons from war.
She rubs her eyes, but there's a lightness
in her head like never before.

So what if the chili left for him
is still downstairs on the table.
No need to go to the door to check.
Isn't the slow soul tune she has
in her head what she used to hear
when he was at home?

Outside Boston on a bus
crowded from the gas crunch
two days before Christmas,
and the kid with the shopping bag
thinks he'll make K.C. in a day.
Bad roads forecast through Cleveland.
The riders' heads, a street of worn
houses puffed with holiday excitement
makes his a neighborhood mistake.
Pure wanderer, eyes closed to sing
a carol. Every place he goes is home.

⌐

In the blue falling light of stereo,
I get a call from home
telling how in the Olds parts plant
when the line shuts down for break
my brother pulls his trumpet out—
Orpheus among the abandoned car bodies—
and he blows:

. . . and Gary been takin' his horn to work—
just blowin' the thing wild at lunch—
and, Chris, you know how Gary can be,
don't matter who's around. but one thing
out on the job they listen to him.
seems everyone, no matter who, if he is
who he is he makes us catch our breaths.
and we start questioning, despite whatever troubles,
WHO'S THIS ANYWAY, *and we push ourselves*
forward like shells, like conches we sing through
to declare the future here. and this beats troubles.
for a while.

Who's this anyway, I mutter to myself,
ain't breath a crazy membership for both nothing
and the unifying wail welling in all things.

⋅⌣

Wait . . . trying to save essences, I sink back in a chair,
imagining Gary with his golden horn—
oblivious, along the assembling line
the right idiom, and his body is a note.
Later, in my dream I see a lone figure

walking through a ruined land.
The birds are all gone and the man is sad.
He is shaking the day's fragments from his head,
and they are flying apart like foreign languages
passing each other, crying out but with no context.
The man has not gotten behind his story
to give what he is to the world as gift.
So sorrow is set to enter the dream
unless one remembers the music of giving:
the underlying quiver, the going over, death, fruit.
The man comes upon a fallen branch.
When he picks it up it is
his arms at his sides extended—
suddenly it's a vast blue flute.
Who can say where the singing starts
but as I dream out-loud, I make myself
connected with the meaning of the figure,
and his words have a radiance which won't be bound
by dream, they ripen in the places for them—
orange, avocado, walker, song, connecting thing.
The singing is my breath but it's not mine—
I give it up in my trivial being.
It is this attitude which glues two realms.

African Sculpture

*After looking at figures from the Baluba tribe at the
DeCordova Museum, June 1979, in Lincoln, Mass. The
sculptures were on loan from Harvard's Fogg Museum
where they were rarely available to the public.*

I am staring out the window
'bout to think something; a nameless
spirit comes through the glass inevitable
as nightfall. This house against the breeze
angles dark as African sculpture
pouting in a museum exhibit.
In the distance silhouetted the ash tree
waves its hand of intricate fingers;
as I trace their bending routes I sense
the flutter of a black-winged bird
flush against my mind's back wall, flying
forward the way that time becomes distinct.
I wonder if it will land out there.
It waves its wing and my blood slowly
ripples. Suddenly, I am negative and it is
scene. I wonder what the pattern is of—
looking out the window at the stars,
my arms reach out to touch their darkest names.
I seem to be remembering something.
I'm about to speak. I might be
a bird's speech where the air is visible
as an old language rising up the throat of
wings, my arms mellow leaves leaning earthward—
but now the traffic outside gears up
and the tree no longer believes in me
and the bird flies off; a strange cold light
shoots its shiny axe thru the sky.

Theory of Curve

"Pitching is just an illusion. You're dealing with a man's eyes. Make him think he's getting one thing, and give him another, and you've got him."

—Al Jackson, pitching coach
of the Boston Red Sox
(August 7, 1977)

Thrown off-center
this string of white
unwinds, cheats some 60 feet.

Then the eye wakes,
rolls down the spine called curve.

Hot patch of pale
burns its ice into kiss of wind and
fear parachuting from chest to waist.
It blurs in type the eye can't read:

a line that numbs
the spine below the belt, the last
of the colored syllables—
someone's got to put it out.

The long parade against busing
stops at Fenway Park. The concessioneer
is a spy who spits in the beer.

High in the bleacher
we cheer for Willie Horton.
He legs a big brown bat.

Lottery

Oh Lord, I need
to win today
of all days.
The cold wind and
damn snow tumble
and not a cornflake
fall to eat, nothing
'cept the flower
of faith to chew, not
a green Uncle Sam.
Rent is due and
temperature low
as one blue eye.
Is that you
listening, Lord?

Lord, I get up
debt-deep in dreaming,
when my ship coming?
My faith, put
long in the land,
owning none, just sweat
and these blood vowels,
and this even trust
in my song, this singing
I am here, no matter
these zero nights,
these eyes looking up—
the sky leaning back
glassy and numb. . . .

Lord, it ain't hard
for you, one nod
from your head
and we right.
No lean faces, no
bare rooms and no
walls to break my stride—
the employment line
steady in a smile.
Play my number
and I'll be over
big yellow moons
and deep drum steps,
I'll be knocking on wood.
Lord, you can do it.

Lord, the blues—
tart as jazz intense
with belief and
loads of laughing too,
but not spending dough.
The roof is leaking—
maybe a sign?
I could see the drops
somewhere else
falling as perfect water
would fall stone from above, so
though I turn away
I have no choice—

Lord, these blues.
Give 'em to the boys
downtown, let me
win their numbers game.

Chosen to Be Water

Across the field the great willow rocking its head
back and forth in the waters of the wind
might mean a hard storm, but who notices?
Suddenly the rain against the westward windows
arrives hard, but honest enough to dictate
the season. Bob Marley is dead today, and
the woman's neighbor aims the bass in his stereo
to match the raindrops' episodic flaring—
but not the dark explosions where they strike
the glass, and not the lament this acid will
etch into the garden which collects it.
She imagines a cabbage out there,
wet, standing against the moist black ground
like a pimple glistening or else a teardrop.
A leaf breaks from it, joining the spill
washed down between rows, and she says, *teardrop.*
Right now the chip on her shoulder is so sharp
she has no need to be disinterested
in pursuing the simile further, as the leaf
flows slowly downhill towards a gully.
She says the fallen leaf is a tear, too.
Suddenly she swears and shakes a sweat off—
squeezes her hips hard while she hums a song.
She wants the bold stroke of intense change.
Music has chosen to be water again.
Is it raining in her neighbor's apartment?
She will go see, and pushes herself up
from a table already wet with her judgment.

Glimpses of Power

I.

Along the road the moon's presence
on the bus into Boston, on the backs of
the mother and child clenched in one
baying they give themselves to,
in the long corridor of night
in the seat ahead where I can't see
but through inertia throw myself to
this otherness before me: a woman,
I guess a single mother with
belly shaped from child, and child—
his body the shape of her longing.

A Black boy. I can see
his reflection in the window—
a 3 year old cosmic thing
crying in his mother's arms
so possessed with some bad pain.
Then suddenly he whirls to me.
I stare the pocks where his eyes are—
see the moon is hidden by clouds.
Pointing out the window up into sky,
he pleads, "fix it, Mistuh, fix it."

And some god in my hand lifts my hand
to touch this child's phenomenal flesh.
Whirling from a seat way back of my self,
I say, "ok," as something intense
in me flies forward, not unlike
stars burning in the sky come forward.

Now the moon descends its distance.
Our eyes are luminous spheres
looking out upon each other, we—
we go floating forward becoming mutual
landscape in our different lives.

II.

That Saturday night at Alice's
new Cambridge house with her roommate
Ruth standing near the empty chair,
holding the wine for the prophet Elijah,
a ceremony, she explained,
"against oppression anywhere—
the Middle East, Chile, Cambodia, Soweto."
And Jew and Gentile alike
question, "why is this night . . ."

Across the room the big piano
left by some prior tenant—
its bench empty except for where
we breathed our words in space
and, above it, how they hovered
holding a grave presence. The room's
hurt air remembering till the walls,
painted over, itched in gooseflesh,
and across time the intense
thuummm of an endless blues, voices
from the losses which have no address.

Alice, what kind of piano is that?

III.

Deep in the forest
quietly watching the leaves fall
the trees drop their hands.

IV.

A psychologist talking to a man at a state hospital
(one of a series of interviews):

Remember how the last time we were talking about the voices
you hear and you said that they were brought about by power,
can you explain that? *No man, you cain't explain no power.* Can
you tell me what power is, what does power do? *Power is force,
it moves things—makes 'em happen.* So power might be, for ex-
ample, a tow truck moving your car? *Naw, that ain't no example,
power is like in the thing, when people talk all crazy—no reason, but
a woman's voice have that dark feeling coming out from her, or a
man's tongue be green—that's the power.* What's power made of
then—is it made of words? *Sometimes, but power is anything with
the spirit—when you can feel a wave in the room or the dog crying
all suddenlike.*

Can you see power? *Sometimes, sho.* Can you show me power? *If
you really want to see it.* I asked you, didn't I? *Yeah, you asked, but
if you ain't just woofin', you be on yo' knees and askin'.*

V.

The pure terror
in the lean angelic body
where the autistic boy kneels on the floor
in the playroom, I pick him up
and he kneels in my lap.

If I shake my keys
his eyes stare together, flashing back
the animal goggled
reflection of a world glimpsed off
where he looks beyond me.

The crusted lips open a moment,
and from the silence his abdication
of this world spills out—
the numbers rhythmically mouthed,
named to the soul of things:
"one two, one two two, one two,
one two two two."

His dark hands that imitate
no one; each separately
shoots out from his body
with the sly orbit of a moon—
flickers up to tap my eyes
where he sees himself flashed back.
For the first time we are real.

Named as number, as thing
at the edge of his ritual, I press
my ears against the flesh
where he touches my head
and realize his counting
as a blessing instead.

    VI.

In the distance
a man going over a hill—
he is the father from childhood.

We are hungry, and call to him,
and run toward the edge
where horizon is—
his hair the quiet burning
crest of a tree on fire.
As he steps down in himself
growing shorter and shorter,
the red of our calling blurs
invisible in the night.
The fire burns out.

"Fuckin' Hinayana."

VII.

On the day of vacation
thinking of the next day's
work, away from work
at the river I stop, nighttime
down along the Connecticut.
The rocks kicked in—
waves slowly becoming nothing
in the dark mirror surface;
and I sing the song heard passing by
a pentecostal church in Worcester—
"to get 'cross the Jordan
swim where you stand.
get on board, lil chillens,
swim where you stand."
In the distance I see myself
stone kicked in: becoming the wave
that becomes the nothing that
signifies. *The Other. All Things. Nothing.*

Ebony plunges in—
her body swimming
her arthritic good legs
and the one bad labrador leg
since her accident.
Pulling herself across the water
a furrow is drawn—
in moonlit water the imagined
line of a fuse
where in her nose
the river explodes.

VIII.

k,
k = 3,
d,
d = 2,
$12 = kd^2$, and $192 = kd^6$,
the series: 3, 6, 12, 24, + . . . +
you, whoever you are,
jumping from number to number.

Speech is wind, when you live
Remember yo' mother's name.
Speech is breath, when you live
Remember yo' mother's name.
Speech is song, if you die
Remember yo' mother's name.
Speech is power, if you die
Say yo' mother's name.
Kah dooom, kah dooom dooom, kah dooom,
Kah dooom dooom dooom.

And Etheridge one night reading the poem
"Ilu the Talking Drum."

Enclosure

After Howlin' Wolf

Mad daddy like mule
kickin' in someone else's stall,
rocks the home's premise.
Knocks at the front door,
teasin' the back door wide,
bends his broodin' voice
in African slang.
Mud-faced feelin' oozes
heart of devilbird,
parts them rural teeth
and blows off steam, a-crowin'
AOH, HOOO, HOOO, HOOOOWEEEE—
so-called back-door man
singin' in his rooster shoes
said, AOH-HOOO, HOOO, HOOOOHEEEE.
Red black daddy cock
puttered in the 70s,
but sixty years of moanin'
dixie bottom blues—
was his prankish testament
how he howled his life.
Love was his calling,
said, *the girls'll understand.*
Spoke his trance-like line,
woke the dollgirl sleep
singin' AOH-HEEE, HOOO, HOOOOHEEEE.
WHA-HEEE, WHA-HEEE, HOOOO.

And when it's all done
the feeling leaves by the window,
rides the last-night dream.
The last guitar line
eeries outside the record—
spirit has no home.

The twelve-bar blues form,
the south, or Chicago,
or some woman's man
never got his number—
a man singin' his wretched roots
never sings at home.

Mud-faced vowels bred
in morning, rollin' along
the road thru his dead age,
chant of distant land
his only closeness. Trance-blue
breath, the drifter's home.

How the Stars Understand Us

". . . because in the dying world it was set burning."

—Galway Kinnell

We are not making love but
all night long we hug each other.
Your face under my chin is two brown
thoughts with no right name, but opens to
eyes when my beard is brushing you.
The last line of the album playing
is Joan Armatrading's existential stuff,
we had fun while it lasted.
You inch your head up toward mine
where your eyes brighten, intense,
as though I were observer and you
a doppled source. In the blue light
in the air we suddenly leave our selves
and watch two salt-starved bodies
lick the sweat from each others' lips.
When the one mosquito in the night
comes toward our breathing, the pitch
of its buzz turns higher
till it's fat like this blue room
and burning on both of us;
now it dies like a siren passing
down a street, the color of blood.
I pull the blanket over our heads
about to despair because I think
everything intense is dying, but you,
you, even asleep, hold onto all
you think I am, more than I think,
so intensely you can feel me
hugging back where I have gone.

Kodac and Chris
Walking the Mutual Landscape

Let's be simultaneous—
you in your sure dogness and me
in my being much as I can muster
knowing there's the forgetful zoo
of being human all about me.
Birth and bombs are far-off business
to these square suburban lawns,
therefore my foot forbidden to sweat
comes down in an anxious shoe.
So let's walk beneath May stars
because for once we both are beings
knowing that we must shit and piss,
knowing nothing lives as a foreignness.

Simultaneous as the weather's feeling,
finding another place for residence—
no neighbor's yard is a boundary.
Don't you got this earth in you?
And I'll be damned if it divides
into yards of different kinds.
Your heart is a boat's blue sail,
so I'll be damned if the grass don't feel
your step is the perfect weight.
First there's nothing and then there's breath,
and then these two shack together.
So I'll be damned if our lives are less—
more the intimacy of both eyes,
more the gift of knot between them.

Animal death, you give yourself to,
and the night around you is monoecious.
So stars materialize as pools of milk—
which is warm-bloodedness and a smile
and the sympathy of a positive belly
with a theorem for a human in its mind.
Now we get near the bad neighborhood
and we must face it as foreground,
deal with it as a presence, a body
to snuggle into and say *yes* to
despite knowing it might wear polyester
or, worse, have words covering every pore.
Frozen faces, doors uptight, shaved lawns—
positive death, so these concrete bits shall rise.

Let's begin being mutual,
you angel moment, you night-light
between houses which are unconnected itches.
Loss is a gap in any process
which humans make a symbol of
by putting their lives at a distance.
Unbroken consciousness whose paw
already touches the goal you move toward,
walk with me and my human devices.
Positive tourist, but I'll be damned
if I don't step down in my neighbors' yards
with my mutt's paw and my situation
whole in the world beneath May stars.

Saturday Morning at the Laundry

Things the way they are
and *things* the way they strive to be:
the yellowperfect, even goldgleaming
on the Sunoco Sign out the window
is not dead plastic and not
some piece flaked from a more perfect place
somewhere else, and not
the yellowness because I say
it's early march and the slant of sun
at 9:18 is right
as I'm sitting in the laundromat
drinking orange spice tea
while my couple of washers is going,
but a chance, a blessing, a beginning—
as a *thing* of this world is, is the use
it will put me to;

so I say *yellow sign, yellow sign,*
obliging this moment with prayer—
kissing the little laughing sun on my lips—
while my voice is falling on things
as yet wordless inside my self,
already golden with the black force
some good god has given to show what is.

       ·ᴗ

You are Lionel, if
when you're twelve
and the dollar-changer swipes the bill
you have to do the family wash with,
and the owner of the joint

like it's none of his business
drives off in his Caddie
leaving you yelling at the air
loud enough to make someone hear,
and it is somehow only the messenger
who lives deeper inside your self
who had planned to go through the world today
clear-headed and wearing sparkling clothes,
who hears, goes to a chair and sits confused
knowing what he had to say
but knowing it can't be loud enough.

More vision than dream, wearing green
and her hair in corn-row fashion,
when the girl walks over to him, a bloom
as the bright red beads in her braids
was the ripeness of the world he had waited for, he needed
to recognize her. A young kid, he wonders
trying to make her a memory of a friend—
someone he knew when he was younger, he thinks,
trying to get on top of the feeling she astonishes with.
So he cannot stop the sudden clouding-over
between them, when they talk the gap
where he is exiled from her and the summer
stuff in her eyes his speech cannot reach,
where the failed part of him refuses to go forward to
her particulars. Her particulars? When he recognizes the region
opened in him by her life, he will get to them.
First, she has her own voice and he must learn to sing
to talk to her: making the usual speech is nonsense—

broken phrases while the washers work, abstract
accidentals they each must will to keep outside their heads.
She knows a carrying-forth, confidently telling she goes
back down to touch the hand of her mother
who has awakened calling her name.
How full of sense the click while they jointly
fold their winged moment of fresh wash—
pants, towels, blouses, sheets, T-shirts,
and her mother's bright *Puerto Rican party dress.* Each item
hanging on its keen label in the mind, so deep
the connection granted, worked-for
despite the washers' arguing. Imagine that.

Chris Gilbert: An Improvisation

(Music of the Striving That Was There)

You, the Piece That Was There

The into was music that said
"be alive" and "willing." As black men
who had found a home in which
our spirits would dance. As not just
flesh, but that indigenous momentum for
entering the truth and being a native
there. On the streets there was word
of a presence. You were among
the throng caught up in the moment.
The beauty of the into
was an attraction free from death,
with a sure mind in front of you
staring back at you and your own
wide eyed nothing in your past.
The list of faces that compose
the word flashed forward, the steady
scrolling of the passing seasons.
You saw Coltrane on the corner—
a lovely sadness looking off into space,
Mahalia a wild attention wailing, "hold on,"
and a recursive Sam Cooke singing
"a change gon' come."
You saw the sorrow in your father's
face flying around in the air,
and in the sunrise's spoiled sphere
your own children's destiny appeared.
You saw an atom shaken free
from the dust scuffled up
as the crowds performed their tasks
in history, and in its make up
you saw a face and, god, it was you.

·- I. STEPS AND TRANSFORMATIONS

Go to a mountaintop and cry for a vision.
    —*Lakota*

Blues/The Blue Case against the Lack Of

Because the raining outside means
let's cover over, over
is a change making status quo
that says the rain will fall
in front of you—fits
in a slick mention of itself
while you seek a gesture
which might measure this rain
and you arrive at tears—
shiny shaped propositions
whose wet patter rises thus
plop plus particular plop
into drops of instance
that you become conscious with;
because the rain come down
down inside, the blue stuff,
mucous conclusions bestowed;
because there is a rain falling
there is no absolute, only
surface rise on top of rise
which is the lack of—love;
because the torrent inward
here those visible words come
raining, that personal repainting;
because the rain going on
your life, a sensitive brown raincoat
because the blue resulting mounts
item misting into bluesy item
until a value at last condenses
as when a lover decides to leave—
first the storm and its quick dark,

the door framing her leaving so
where she walks off and into
the smaller hard-to-make-out-things
beyond your neural canvas.
Now you feel that vague
focus an inner rain brings
and you say, "yeah," not
because the rain is deeper
but its veneer turned more serious.
And you, up all night, praying,
"baby, baby, baby, please,"
saying, "I'm a painter, baby,
and I wanna draw yo' face.
I'm a painter, mornin',
and I wanna draw yo' face.
yo' presence is a blessin',
and yo' image is a taste."
Because this is blue because
you sing and sing and sing.

The Art of the Improvisers

On my fourth try I get through
from Providence to 'GBH
with my answer to the quiz
the DJ sitting in for "Eric
in the Evening" has posed. Outside
the whipping winds' hiss matches
the telephone's sound in my left ear
as I hear my neighbor opening
the door to enter the building
in my other, reminding me it's
February. Cracking a story
on her student who has a goal
to be taught to play well
as Tatum, Dorothy Donegan
is the guest on tonight's show.
"Rosita," which is Spanish
for my mother's name, is the sound
that I hear before the door bangs
shut behind the neighbor. The guy
who brought Ms. Donegan in is trying
like a cop to have her be
a commodity the upscale Boston
audience can take, but she talks
about grits. Another record
goes on while the DJ flusters
searching for something to say.
"Rosita" is the image
I coax back into consciousness where
its music wavers, coming and going,
so I could believe there's a rose
outside dancing against the white

whistle of the midwinter wind—
dark, iridescent, with a cup
that gives up like the opened stop
of an instrument deep music—
because of the way my mother's fierce
resolve always seemed the meaning
of her name. "Rosita,"
six callers correctly phone in
to win the free tickets before me,
"the first Coleman Hawkins version."
When the DJ is busy with a
call, the resourceful Ms. Donegan
improvises a jazzy faux pas
by going into an explanation
about how her band's money is split.
I'm on the line with my answer
to the DJ's question
just for the hell of it.

Joseph Walking Light's Way Out of Time

*(adapted from a story told me at the
Rosebud Community, South Dakota, 1992)*

My quest is to reach the plain atop the hill.
Some weeping to be done to reach that land.
I have done wrong in my time up till now.

I want so much, my Lord.
I had forgotten the dust, and how to walk on foot.
Someone throw the earth thru my heart.

I need to get lost in the tall grass,
under the tree with a vulture in the sky above it.
Don't pity me, don't pity me.

No sleep for four days, I
must swallow for seven thought on top of my mind.
I must take the stars into me to let my vision widen.

Building a campfire, I sweat a stream.
When the coals darken, I see
moon in which the rice is laid to dry.

Myself, I am seeing what I see.
Myself, I am the wind before the wind.
My quest is to see myself as the wind.

My Lord, you are a big eyeball
turning out there, naked with the lid open.
My soul is a clear tear because of all you see.

Now I am a night sky walking on two legs.
I have no private life—
My quest is to continue and to end.

I say good-bye to silence.
I say good-bye to everything,
even my weeping words.

My one step is homage.
My other has nothing to do with what I know as a man.
I stumble onto the trail of holiness.

The path is a flower that opens.
I see a hole with the world inside it.
I step into the circle in the middle of this scene.

Soweto, the Present Tense

By the power lines, their long
catenaries dipped with copper,
we stop at the clearing mid-June
in the patch of sorrel and grass
and watch how the telephone
cables trail off in the talk
between sender and receiver.
Farther, we find a city paper,
the stories breaking into black
and white patterns on the page,
the news blowing bad and bitter.
The news is the codes themselves,
strange absences always adding up
silently, like it never matters
the consciousness Biko brought
beaten into *just black names*, pithed pieces the
word the earth's dark skin the letters the
language didn't think proper—
signs for its complexion or its state.
I am reading between the lines, how
ululating Zulus uttering blood
is a message that carries weight.
After this this afternoon under the wires
the dark outlines will sag towards each other
like closing sides of a drawbridge.
My friend will pick and eat some sour grass
and listen to the humming overhead,
will lean where the utility poles
press in the earth from this weight.

The Atmosphere

An Indian woman looking older than her age stops me in the middle of the square. "It's for the kids," she says, when she asks me for money, as she points to a teenaged boy and girl sprawled against the wheels on the side of the van stopped farther up the street. "Got no money 'cause the white man got it," she says, "you understand, brother." The kids seem to be taking all this in, though they never raise their heads: the boy embarrassed to be present, the girl drooping her head drowsily like a plant that has not yet risen with morning. I'm wondering where the woman has come from. Her face is gray. Her eyes would be soft and look deep, but what stands out are her wrinkles and her pebbled skin. Her long facial lines are saying something like when one is mentioned to by the atmosphere from its record in rock. I'm beginning to feel this is some kind of hustle until the woman gives me the last plastic rose she has left. Then she just walks off. I put it in my shopping bag. What else can I do with a rose on my way back to work.

Beneath the florescent lamp from a vase on my desk the rose looks disheartened and sad. Its shape sags like an old woman's flesh. Yet the plastic seems to pulse with a bursting-into-itself inner stirring as though it were a wave. It reminds me of a woman I saw once who froze in the middle of the street as she waited for an onrush of cars to hit her. Then she suddenly burst into shrieks. Something about this rose is haunting me so I know I cannot throw it away. In my dream tonight I am the boy bending over the rose's corolla when the plastic darkens and the petals start falling, one after another, slow mo.' I become the young girl shrieking. Though I can't make out what it is she would say, I sense it is something the old woman would say. Now I am running frantically beneath the falling petals, cupping my hands to catch them. Rubbed against my fingers, they feel like soft eyelids, each with a tear on its inner side.

The Turn

Back home, the cornbread and
collards cook upstairs, smelling
of years ago, purifying
the black basement air
up our noses in a high.
You pack the pool balls together
into the rack, cracking them
like they were bones and your whack
would free a dream holed up inside.
I break balls, then inhale—
the pattern in the air so
poised, it shows the shape from
our young selves to this new now
that we've become that
peers back here at what we were.
Coltrane on the stereo snorts
the dream of his last album
into notes—*Offering, Expression.*
We share my Schlitz and talk how
everybody from the old neighborhood
is stricken with the wages from
working in this reservation
where every brother is afflicted
in the man's mental jail
because we end up buying his shit:
the Jheri curl, the crossover
step that the ten percent do,
the failures to make community,
the sad marriages, the visionless
work, the nothing to look forward to
living that we all stand in line to do.

But here the room is tranced now
with the sweetsmell of some of leftovers
heating upstairs. Our stomachs tuned
outward are twin moons singing—
the attitude is low tide.
Across the table from me my same
brown muscles etched newer
on my brother's arms, the same sweatshirt
heartbeat rolling back the sleeves.
Now the balls spread out in stars'
patterns, a moving sublime.
The black ball is like coal
I wish I could squeeze down
beyond a coal to make a crystal,
be the shell that would hold
my reflection there, then be
the seeing from the reflection
that looks with curiosity back at me.
We listen—the purging amidst
the chaos in Coltrane is being
a steadfast improvisation to
silencing this reservation time.
Birth, death, the ephemeral:
Breath breathed into a story
that tells us we are lives
just for its vanishing season.
Now you break the stillness of four balls
bunched near the far pocket, a geometry
selflessly unfolding.
Then like someone going away
or a wise child on his birthday

seeing himself as candle
lit and blown out and lit
again each year, you pass
the cue to me and motion it's my go;
the roll of your shot still gliding.
In this moment we imagine
we are the motion of these spheres.
Their perfect whirl forward is living.
For a moment I go backwards, wishing
I could see my original growing up
again. For a moment I expect to find
the spirit here that was here
in illo tempore. For a moment I expect
to resurrect that passing through whose proof was
a period used up in time. For a moment
while the nothing comes I am nothing
till I purge the pass from this taking place
that is me—the present depository:
the sound of Coltrane scaling
the upper range of a wall in the dark.
My body is this room crowded
with the image of this room.
Above the table the light bulb
swings in vanishing arcs
where you've brushed it
waving the tip of your cue.
Now the egg-shaped shadows
beneath the balls swing in response,
picking the oblong signals
from this low-watt light. We watch
like we don't care, Coltrane's thinking

is the sound of a big wheel
spun around so perfectly
it is a moon orbiting itself.
In shifting light we ebb and surge
and surge and break in grin
when the black ball misses the hole.
Hearing that upstairs dinner is done
moves us to a different mode.
And we laugh at this game.

Bad

Things are bad because in their core
is written the bad word whose voice
other things turn toward or away from

into the unimpeachable meaning
wine, rose, Willie—and
by those names act!

The word itself as a thing
neither lying nor not
but speech punctuating space

unretrievably uttered
objectivity whose calling
spells the deep wind of nothingness

the understanding without a word
the language without a claim
the speech of the dreaming things

the drunk arrested for cussing his luck
the silence before a storm driving a voice to prayer
the nameless hunger in the cities which never gets addressed

the old blues man in the nightclub
singing or crying it's all the same
it's all for nothing, which

when I'm right I am the words
I am
the symbol in front of me
myself
where nothing is ahead of me
the wind.

Someday I will name a thing
so real it won't need saying
the angel who lives inside
who beats my lips into shapes
will be a wife to me
as though to name a thing
is praying to a force
or else fucking it up.

On the Way Back Home

           It's a different world
now that we've found a doe dead, against
a late fall background crystalled with frost, steaming
still, in the middle of the two-lane as it goes
where the forest starts going west of the city,
while the feeling is as we hover hushed over her,
everything dark except for the florescent white
flashlight beam sheeming back from the various sleek
facets of her sad and useless beauty, she was
one of us though more like a fallen star
the three of us had wandered to to witness,
her otherness a light from her eyes facing up
went nowhere, was all there on itself
existing as an end in itself, instructive so
we couldn't follow it but were compelled—
like refugees awaiting our turns to be
an absence happening, a promising effect—
to turn our gaze onto our absent selves,
to turn our attention into a thing
to inspect, and from this focus point, go out
wandering in our various directions.

A Passage

From the road we see the skeletal stalks
of the corn from summer, forms so anguished thick
with August, they rot into their spaces—
a beauty whose only sign is the shadow
cast by the sorrow of the autumnal light. Love,

from this view there's inside the field's surface
a swaying where the wind whooshes through, a
presence like the impulse passing through
a rippled pond or old black church
people who at-the-end turn their lives into humming.

Love, we are an edge to this field, our bodies
border to rows standing six feet tall.
What I wish for you is this momentary sense:
the picture is of something perfect
like standing in line for nothing.

Gazing presences, however long we stand here
we are extending a line. The summer is
a passage that sees itself through us
just as on the road for a moment we see
ourselves changed as ever we needed to be.

Tourist

(The Robert Frost Place—Franconia, New Hampshire)

Because it is the route that is the work
you could take the world itself to mean
yourself. Into these hills you've taken to
like the present, you could take place and be one
with the subject of your feeling arising
before you. The way the Queen's lace sways
could be an indication of your breath
coming and going. As if an outline for time
itself, here I am stepping forth as an instance
walking the mountain road to the hilltop where
around the bend I'll hear someone working
on the house the frame of whose part—the material
and the aesthetic and their perishing—linked
together will stand for history. It is
July, the goldenrod drooping heavily
at the road's edge, the daisies all over
exploding with white rays, the coltsfoot buttery,
and nodding thistle rose-purple everywhere
itself, the little water in the wind
all at once reminding me of myself. I am
into small steps here—I total the bits of me.
I have lived in countless places, childless,
without song, and now no church of time ahead
behind whose doors one can walk and be
transformed, enormous, again, and facing the sky.
I am nearing the end of my youth, not
nearly the person I thought I would be
not half my life ago, when life's sure, blind
ubiquitous outbreaks of energy for *doing*
something searched for a home for the empathy

that would be me, Armstrong walking the nearer
moon and me hot headed, twenty, with
a future seeming never too soon, seed
whose crazed circumstance among things yielded
its mysterious blossoming. Now the people
passing me in the cars, faces red and
pink swollen like the climbing bittersweet
berries, bouncing up and down like dice
in trustless boxes, might just as well be me
caught in a body nowhere completely
at home. The little water in the wind
reminds me of my sorrow, a quick gust
I can't explain. What is happening is me
even as I see the bee balm's bright star
call the hummingbird into its circle,
even as every doubt I am is my flowering
home that you have called me into, world.

Watermelon

As I walk up to you, you are like the silence after one word and the spasm of the next. Your skin envelops a boundless love. Because of your surplus there is no jealousy anywhere in you. A mother's belly in the ninth month; you make me feel so proud. Whenever you're ready, I'm ready.

You are a planet on this planet. Laying here on the warm ground, your only dream is to swallow the sun. You make the earth behind you the mellow heavens. The red inside you is the summer's ripest day. You are a sweet impulse, a wet word. You are more than a mouthful.

When I take you to my thirst, I can't say enough about you. I spit out the seeds.

Getting Over There

(Outside Mendocino)

That that that all day the vulture overhead was
screeching at in long resignation like naming
something not happened but always here
down here where dusk has begun covering
everything is even more a mystery,
even more a place whose passages deepening
lead to a way beyond testament tonight,
tonight after all day talking those small talk
things till talk was just a loud grasping
without any reaching, till what came forth
was the risk when the tongue goes random and
finally resorts to regarding the world as "whatever."
I get lost in the middle of all this "naming
this is chaos," this abyss as far from use as
the trance of the these hills in their ecstatic silence
or as the grace of the deer encased
out here in their proud bodies, whose proof is
the needlessness they show as they pass
without comment beyond this midsummer dust
into the air's dark innocence which is
an endlessness and a death everything comes to.
Now as I climb the old logging roads in the redwoods,
trying to get to a clearing between the treetops,
flashlight so small that it leaves a starry presence,
cedar scenting the air and mountain flowers
which would blaze into colors if this were daylight,
I follow a dried-up stream along so it becomes
the paths, doing this uphill dance, sweet dew on everything
and sweat on me, till whatever this is I am is
out of breath, till I can't say "whatever" or
will not because in my bliss it's nothing that I mean.

II. WITNESSES OF THE STRIVING THAT WAS THERE

Lord I rolled and tumbled,
cried the whole night long.
       —*McKinley Morganfield*

Willie's Fake Book

Once, in a dream,
                    a twitch
trembled through the fabric, woke
the ghost in it, who, aroused, took his turn
walking the world
                    a face among the anonymous multitudes
numbed in documentary of daily life,

waxing burlesque in community at the mall
with the man on TV, moving his lips
                                        to the lips
he watched with the sound turned off, while they said
"there is nothing to be done," while the intrepid screen images
went on in conspicuous commitment,

lamenting the Charlie Parker imitators
in mythic sameness, he heard the John Coltranes
on tape instead of John Coltrane, and was moved to dance but

not to it but the blitzy ethos from a boombox
in harmony with cartons, a pile of dogshit, bottles, scattered
potato chips and, while standing in that midst,
came to rhetoric as a cartoon—a dialect
framed in superhero pimp costume and chains that could not fit,
    yelling
at his woman friend, "I own you
                                        bitch," as a lithe schoolgirl,
not yet pubic, vigilant; waiting for her bus, witnessed
and had her tongue imprinted with all this, then

shouldering his own history, he read
the disquiet when the writer proclaimed,
"there is nothing left to write," and suffered
the notion of art as a changing notion—
and sensed the smile forming, imperceptibly,
on John Singleton Copley's *Head
of a Negro* on exhibit,

and, then, finally ran into the fake that he is, on a corner,
using his routine-sweet, streettalk to hawk T-shirts
stenciled with the accidents of the alphabet, woven
together into this lyric:
*My God Is the Authentic
I Will Not Make a Church of It,*

then misread this and all his steps to mean:
*To Witness Is to Be But a Bit
But Suffused with the Authentic,*
who, then, with this honest list of woes and turns
devised in the neighborhood, hypertensive
solos originally transcribed, pure
swollen, black man pulsing through his veins, arose.

Pleasant Street

Playing cultural solitaire in Worcester near Newton Square, I'm
the ersatz narrative clerk, doing time on a block where I am
the only black and all my neighbors swear in a Greek or Irish
        brogue
that their fathers rode here on the *Mayflower.*
Across the street in the country's first public park
the city fathers' misanthropic sons lose their way
to the local high school. Honor students at angel dusting,
they become literati gouging graffiti onto the trees.
Staring back from the broken bottles littering the ground
they become the beautiful people glistening here—
darling debris glittering in the grass. A short walk down
the old Swedish area that Charles Olson grew out of is, now,
a margin to his instant, a feeling on the senses *like*—
a shadow's effect on those days where there was no sun.
I'm blind from the tan on the skin of his archeological children.

I am in my thirties in the 1980s where
it's suddenly very hip to remember that you did *that*
or you did *this* to each of the old 60s Motown hits,
where in the personals, "service consultants" will advertise
to sell you memories to swear that you were there.
You find this gone experience everywhere you go—
in the decade's drugs and the fashions from the fifties.
Living this way where nothing is at stake, the "I" is somewhere
else.
The whole country is a commodity the government advises,
so the prostitutes downtown, serious civil servants, follow this
dictum down to the trick. The line for all this is
the line, meaning *go with the flow* or what is real is whatever
a sign buys. Its value, more or less the appearance

of *their* language. Even the smock my priest neighbor wears
is a brand he buys to say the right thing. At the store

on the corner I buy the *Boston Globe,* and mornings chat
with the druggist, thirty years my senior, a repository
talking about his younger days. When he rings my sale
he disses my dollar as he gives me tales about the times.
Cussing the news through his long Jewish vowels which craze us,
a revolutionary disrupting the symbolic order,
with his excise he covers my paper so that he can rap
to his public—as if in our speech the USX on the front pages
becomes, across town, US Steel again—just like that.
Caught up inside in good talk, we can hardly forget
how our subject splits, while the twin screaming signs of Amoco
and Exxon bitch at what's happening outside that language is
the cheapest thought going, while the traffic on Pleasant Street,
a parade of impatient MBAs, pushes on downtown to the bank
and its wages.

A Sorrow since Sitting Bull

Dust on the horizon,
whirlwind, whirlwind blown
in the globe of your eye
where you sit in the back
of the pickup, facing back,
with your reservation a skin
surrounding you, with a warm Bud
in your hand, with the where
the dirt road leads beneath you
spun up as the wheels spin around
till the present narrows to nothing
at the horizon.

The yankee shops everywhere—
like a ring around your life—
sell beadwork, jade, bottled spirit.
Dust on the horizon, you wait
for a wind to bring the buffalo back.
Nothing comes, not even a job.
A gust circles here in lament.
It doubles, reading in the gut
of the grasses that have become this road:
*All Your Relations Are Ghosts
in the Truck with You*, faithful you,
facing back, facing back.

Absentee Landlord

A dog's bark breaks the December
ten-degree weather, a bitter dark
space bleaching into a voweled ache
that staccatos the thin wind, fuzzes
into consciousness as a hurt.

A cry ballooning in the surface
of things, it's like the residue
of city air left in the lung,
while you search these suspenseful streets—
the houses, snowmen holding their tongues.

At the boundary between buildings
the fence rattles its steel scream,
as you peer in an iced-over window
and swear the owner must be absent
since he lets you take his absent signs,

be a prophet for all that he means.
While the wind, which holds our worry,
whistles wild, while the dog barks
himself out, when you look in the glass
and feel yourself in the view as a part,

you are now the subject of this scene.
Become the symbol of what you've framed,
or else don't change. Be nothing
like the dead, be the absentee
who will not attend what he means.

The "The"

At closing time,
standing outside the public library
with ID card expired,
the books remain on shelves—
Lev Vygotsky, Toni Morrison, Levertov, Cassirer,
and the Zora Neale Hurston (which probably isn't there),

an allegorical reader
imagines the words in
public library
as "everything which is locked up"
        in quotes.

I feel like some third person
locked outside the language
through which I am
the things I mean.

To them who want to hide
my face, I say
my body is a display
of truth as I put it
where it belongs—
in the public domain.
I say this loudly and bawdily,
I say this out of place.

·כ

9 p.m. in January the sky refuses,
then breathes its cold holding
slap across my face, and
the dead spot in the starter motor
where the car won't do
            wheezes,
in hand holding key the frozen
failed juice of synapse crying.

You give up (the lights in library closing,
the words in library—theirs),
you give up, desert the car,
its prophylactic comfort—
till in this baptized dark with lips chapped shut

feet starting up stamp a distinctive
            scrunch, scrunch, message-making music toward home,

till there between steps, where the hard inner sides
of the snow squashed together
merge in a chorus of moaning—
till I swear I hear my unmade
footsteps gesturing ahead of me
as a mark of forward memory,
"ain't gon' let nobody turn me 'round."

        ·~

Afraid that I am rapist
a white woman hunches
when I pass, turns her head to a numb

kind of other
where nothing I could think is kind
but in-
trusion. My thoughts puke up
        incognate.

Later, in a shop window's mirror
the dark face there is penetrating, heartless
hollering—
till out of fear I, too, turn away.

        ˙ᴗ

Walking home I am a
you you you you you, a
bad dream I, too, am not into—
the "the" that my loving refuses
to own, as I try to place
myself among the facelessness, forms
whose abused use reduces
even my own bodily truths
to a mask of inhuman mass.
So the boy snowballing a bus
while his German shepherd menaces
is an urchin from an urban
Wyeth scene, while the hordes of
the homeless harangue and harass,
and the wise ones of the streets
put off made useless people till crazy
and the neighbors are apart, and a part
of me tries to ignore it all,

till out from a pack
of the prematurely dead
huddled in a doorway
comes this grasp which is not
a thing I can turn into a name—
a ghost hand from a man
who says he's Lazarus,
who quotes Langston Hughes, whose black
body is so black it's pre-
African, it's purple, it's bruise
set on a set of bones,
as he laughs between poems
and the gaps in his teeth,
and offers me a swig
from his bottle of wine choked
inside a greasy McDonald's bag,
till, walking further on, I realize
that I, too, can, through myself, just be,
realize that a man can move beyond images
and "what ain't so" into the great gulf
of what ain't talked about,
realize that that man's sudden gesture
is the "the" in this
language that doesn't get said
and that I must name it
to have it live as part of me.

Its Meaning: The Grace to fill myself
with the silence of the other world
and have it be the thing.

Andy Warhol's Marilyn as Nigger

           is layers whose
fields of color de-
compose into x-rays so
the figure becomes a "colored" ghost,
a background and not
as conscious as its consequences: the quick
picture, no
brush strokes or texture, no
sharp lines, depth, or mystery
attitude, only surface,
                  the litho lipsticky—
but not resistant, the rabid space
streamlined to the cortex,
a visual quickie.

The face covered up with light and red lines
in polished pin-up becomes this
practice: someone's paint
is sweating hung on the walls
of the repetitious container,
the American mind. Someone else's
impression is hot but dulled in
its repetition, shallow dreams shallow
glaring from these flat frames, and
what is clearest is never said—
this is a picture of
the painting: the
screened print or photo,
he gives to you this
                personality,
you wear it to death.

"I am what I think I am. You are what I think you are."
—LeRoi Jones (Amiri Baraka)

". . . every limit presupposes something beyond it."
—Vladimir Nabokov

Wall

no one has ever held me
like i wanted, the exact measure
of my length.

　　·‿

i am so cold
i am the color of the smooth white stone
in the womb; i refuse osmosis.
i have no name
but the name of the day ahead,
here I come tomorrow.
if my mother calls i don't answer
i am stubborn i like it my way.
across veins she travels a dark river
but i'll be firm i will be firm.
when our eyes meet she sees stone
stone.

　　·‿

my father is joy but so far gone
he is infinite.
a distant point wherever he is
between him and here

i extend his line.
i am the little touch of death he etches
with his numb hands the banished place
outlined in my mind a thing
separate from myself and not living
either.

꜆

my thought the sign keep off the grass,
beware the dog, closed, do not enter,
but still the pure one come here—
oh wow connecting language.
i say what he writes on me,
"I USED TO BE THE SURFACE OF WATER
BUT REALLY I'M ITS DEPTH, BELIEVING I'M TOPS."
he feels he press
"I THOUGHT I WAS PRIVATE PROPERTY
BUT REALLY AM THE VOICE OF GOD
TURNED AWAY AND FEATURELESS, MARK MY
    WORDS."
he jazz he june
"I THOUGHT I WAS A GHETTO ROOFTOP
BUT MORE THAN THAT I AM
WHERE THE MOON LOOKS DOWN SHINING
COME ON, WE'LL FLOAT THE NIGHT TOGETHER"—
though he speaks the close folk voice of brother
or sister hands linking mine in chant
i must be different
i will not sing his songs—
i'll wait until november when i'm gray.

i am the voice of limits i must
interrupt this fun.

　　　·ᴗ

you and i are always apart—
we are like two languages.
i almost hear your singing—
yours is a strange tongue
and me a word it will not kiss.
if i approach you keep your distance—
language only goes so far.
mine is a flat tongue.
i think i want to sing to you
but there are so many words
and all indifferent they can not matter,
they can not think about
but how one measures absences.
you are on their other side,
a quiet word i can not speak inside of
i can not be your words.

　　　·ᴗ

all these thoughts i have
are small steps come back to myself—
even this i hesitate saying:

　　　·ᴗ

you are what i stop short of

Straight Outta Truth

Even when the light at the corner change, no one move. Every-body be standin like fearin to be called. Them who move move like a storm got own they sense, like hearin a call—even they own names—be like lettin in mo wind till the gut gon rush from they sense to they heart and they be stone. No wonder we huddle on these corners. We bunch up by our looks, but the name on the forehead don't tell what the body gon do beneath. At all the corners we hang out like a handful of stars been thrown into constellations. But nobody readin what we sayin. We bunch in all kinds of shape, some weepin and some rejoicin, some in coffins and some in carriages, some in silks and some in shackles. Some hunch over like shy boys who wanna walk in a locked closet and hide. Nobody look up. No one seein nothin. The ones called to-morrow be like glass. The horizon comes up clear as Compton through they guts. A cloud of hammers hangin over they heads. Nobody wanna be called truth.

The "Joe" people work in the windowed buildings near the cor-ner done also found a way to gettin round they self. They make up the charge for the cost of frozen food. They make up ways to make you buy a new washin machine. In they walls of they building they make other walls cluster together. Like these walls be they wretched selves. They pattin each other on they back like "you're doing a great job there, Joe, staying in your box." Every new Joe get a desk inside a cluster. It come down from they bossman that the desk be a used one worked by a ole Joe help the new Joe feel broke into his job. He sit behind his desk, and the desk stand in front of him like a ticket-taker. But nobody be readin what he meanin. Nobody don't notice that the build-ing don't learn. Every floor of the building froze into a company mask. The mask don't look outside.

Every day a face come to us through TV. The face beam down from a high up distance to say it be harmless. It say I'm wit you, Joe. Might be a personality speak, but my name ain't Joe. The people who live next door might be, though. They leave they TV on through the night. In they house it never be all the way day or all the way night—just the kind of light yo eyeball sense when someone else thumb pressin against it. Nobody never see nothin in this light. Nobody be saying what the nothin sayin. Like the look need a name of, say, the brother full enough with oh-don't-i-feel-good-this-morning that when he look down he already seein his shit on every corner. Alive enough he divide his body in small squares of skin and give them each to us like a charm to save us from our terribleness. As a face we fly outside our self to feel the weather. A knower who know it ain't the cold we fear but our claim on each other. A spirit-u-all to fix our claims to-gether into one piece. Right now fear of the cold keep us huddled near home. We shoot at the wind. Fear everywhere. The mask on TV wince, then stick out its tongue when it find it is not hit.

Zeus Getting the Last Word

Zeus had gotten tired of thinking about himself so he decided, "time to get married." To find himself in the middle of a new feeling, not bothered by himself in the old modes of being who he was. His goal was to have someone that he could be a revelation to—fresh, clear, and prior to. Soon he made up the idea of the foreigner, something that had never happened to him. The goddess that he conjured up to marry was his opposite, say, a poet—and Chinese. On the night following the wedding ceremony Zeus insisted that things could not be consummated unless his bride declare her purity, otherwise the act would lack. He needed to know that in some guise he had not before had access to her. This was the demand he desired for transparency. But as part of the set-up for the marriage Zeus had made himself forget Chinese, so that his bride would truly be foreign to him. As a result the goddess had to seek some symbol as a substitute for the language which would not work with him, as a power to pull her forward from the future in which he had deferred her. In the earth in front of him she began fashioning gestures of pure thing—stones, flowers, fish—anything to serve as root. So they both were trapped—always the goddess yielding symbols of herself, and then symbols of those symbols, and the god never understanding.

And so it has come down from the gods that all speech is a claim for transcendence, an attempt to step forward from one form—absence—into the pure plane of difference. And so it has come down that all poetry leads to more poetry. And so it has come down that one must choose between getting things as they are or getting the last word about them.

A Woman's Boat Adrift in August

The image is anybody which
will not sail as it has
traveled on summer days
swirled in salubrious silk—
a small blue freedom billowing
with the healthy breath in the sky,
but tonight my mind is clotted
with replicas of Hiroshima
photos, as my feeling drowns
while I kneel and pray to protect
against the world the candle
flaming in this little wooden boat
I've fashioned to let fly
at the pond's edge dirty
with the city's rot and rubbish,
as my head corrupts
even as my living drifts
out across the trap of the trash
to the flat black face staring up
through the worry of these waters.

Today I passed some spray-painted
hated signs on my way to work, those racial
"ABCs," slides, illuminating
in my head a new wall of grief.
And I was working through the name
of the damned ones for August when up popped
the x-rayed white one with the baby
burned in the bombing. It flashed on me
that this future now is a mask
whose grimace is so grotesque

I can only protest by praying
to its fruitless gods—paper cup,
plastics, wrappers, prophylactics—
to ward off my wearing it.
Tell me of a sanctuary
where I can walk beyond my me
and be, not to have sorrows
as I wander out from shore,
as the memory thing stares up at me.
Here the carp, seeing my figure
as a generous sky which lies,
descend into deeper water.
And the shell of my boat atop
the water is afire like facsimiles
of Hiroshima in the movies.

Beef (with Symbols)

I get to the campaign rally and "fuck,
there's no mo chicken," but the candidate,
the divine Mr. Sound Bite, stops eating his
long enough to cite some wrongs and cluck,
"there'll be soon be beef for each and every plate."
And about the lack of cole slaw, he promises
that more is coming with Cokes aplenty,
and music to help us all do the *trendytrendy*.
It was your usual day, and so forth,
with God on someone's side. But where my man
flunked the test was thinking that I'd give a damn.
I want food, relevant tack from a bottomless source.
A meaty word to last me past the hassle
of this symbol spewing more symbols out like an asshole.

Untitled

She was the first to say it. She said the sound of the sounds for names, verbs, all-matter-of-things-green sticking up through the snow, patches of uncovered blue-black earth sort of sexual wet where the sun had been, dog barking, books, yesterday and to-morrow, Plato and Fanon and the differences between them, the names of the letters spelling coffee on the bottle of coffee brandy. We were walking through the woods, the path around the lake with the smell of leaves preserved from fall and with the smell of joggers' sweat. She named these two, "grace" and "masturbation." Because death was in both these smells I felt that they were the same thing. If it's death, she insisted, the death which rises with absence, yes, but then accepts itself like knowing we are not in heaven but walking around a lake with an abandoned bathhouse over there beautifully washed in sun. This was the death she meant. Because she was an artist she arranged everything into a new order, and she was the guide. Thus she pointed out loon, pine needle, lichen, and potentilla: 1, 2, 3, and 4. Because I was momentarily infatuated the order seemed natural. And when she shrugged off spelling *Hiram Walker* the brandy I drank with her was a general kind but coffee even more. With this wild stroke she believed she was working on the problem I was having with seeing the simple beauty in things. She wanted me to have the specific sense of what we were doing so that I might recognize her. I could tell by the far-off look on her face that she was begin-ning to feel I would never yield far enough. The uneasy sense that we would stay two versions of ourselves, never addressing fully ourselves. She felt that I felt she wasn't there—at least not in the complete way she had felt herself when she melted snow in her mouth and in the melting loved the taste of spring, felt herself in the center there. It was a need she had to show me something— sweet, powerful, sincere—that would overcome the way I was looking past what we were doing to try and locate some ideal truth. We made love against the warm side of the bathhouse. I saw pictures, a flood of memories from summer days as a boy pulling up dandelions, finding robins' eggs in spring. Afterwards when we talked it was as if it were the same. It was as though she were showing me a notice sign, *this is life*, like—"oh, someone left his watch, do you see the mallard out there, what do you think of Reagan's talk about making the Sandinistas say uncle, Reagan's such an asshole." After that things went more slowly. As though we'd temporarily reached a deep place we both were inside of, could call across to touch each other. I was infatuated. Because she was a biologist she arranged everything into a new order. Walking again we found a set of tracks in the snow; she said she could picture the animal who'd left them. We lost these tracks in a bare spot but up ahead found another set—this time bigger and deeper into the white which was a little page-like. She began describing the animal—it had a gold furry coat, a Chuck Berry face, and big blue fins for swimming, it was like the animal I was when riding my bike when I was five and sure I was beginning to get off into flight. She said these new tracks were more dreamy and impressive than the first set, that they belonged to a special animal. I disagreed. "They're both the same," I said, shaking my head in the air. "Or at least, the same animal made both sets of marks." Now she was getting annoyed with me, "why wouldn't I let things be what they might be, and, well, this was my loss." We went on arguing. She brought up the raccoon that I had told her had wandered onto my porch last night. "Let's say the raccoon made tracks of different kinds," she said, "then why not three types, or five, nine, and so on. Your raccoon wouldn't make much sense—or, anyway, our idea of the shapes of its paw wouldn't. You've just ended the faithfulness between the life of the raccoon—its late-night tramp across the road to sniff flowers, gnaw on old bones, knock over the garbage cans—and the place in our own lives for it, our knowledge of it. And I don't know why I go on talking to you anyway. You don't really hear me. It's as though you're cutting the bond between my words and what I mean." And suddenly she was going to cry. I imagined what it would be like to cut the tie between the word and its world. Just the sound of calling the white pine red pine, the rock—ice, or just the sounds themselves. I tried to imagine her argument. *Raccoon crouched down, blacken eyes falling back, drawing its fat drum of a body across the snow, furry inkling a manual of style— distinctive midnight cat.* I shut up, drank the rest of the brandy. What she said was music.

Society's Heroic Underdogs

Below the city the subway is a womb in which the innocent boy is sitting on his stoop with his head in his hands. The baby's first needs are centered largely on the functions of the body. A baby will tell you what it wants and when—mostly by different kinds of crying. Oh glorious hunger that through the blue soon drives the hour drives the redneck when; mad wants that ride the teenage train ride baby even lower.

Baby is doing just what many police departments do when they set up sting operations. He romantically sees people as either victim or outlaw, struggling for dignity and self worth, but with little direction. Your voice is a type of body contact, so do talk to baby. But speak quietly with a soothing and reassuring tone of voice. Don't move suddenly since this startle him. Remember he is as innocent as a police department.

The boombox reported that he was born in the USA. He got into a little hometown jam, so they put a rifle in his hand. The story noted, in a remark voiced by several speakers, that the advertisements being issued by the chief of staff are about more than a political counterrevolution, they are cultural signs as well. One speaker cried out, "I am the other." Somebody else cried, "I am somebody." While the wheels of the subway car cried out their arrival, no one noted the sudden shit going down.

The fields of repeating words blossom into a truant thoughtfulness below the city. But when the body is full of erasure, the bottom falls out. Oh glorious what that must be spoken to softly. Oh romantic sting that drives the stimulus in a tunnel through the skin dries the mouthing stream, blasts the gastric blood, dries those mouthing cries. Oh barren arrival, oh crooked worm. Oh, news reports. Oh glorious remark. Oh, baby will poop out, "Boom, boom, boom. Boom, boom, boom."

*"Then make a program for X that will make
. . . X's states act just like Y's. Once that's
done, X's behavior will look
exactly like Y's . . ."*

—Marvin Minsky

For Instance, Genealogy

Each morning, I
read the "Living Section"
of the *Globe* and the *Times,*
pondering them.
I stare into
the situation
involving the faces
in a photo
till it's right
and proceeds and embraces
me. I
act "like"
this is me.
Sort of like
the awakening
had by Derrida
in reading Nietzsche
as his own
Thing. Sort of
like being
Nietzsche. Sort of
like being
Derrida. Sort of

like being
a personality.
This is like
Robert Morris's "Site"
with Carolee Schneemann
the refugee
figure doing the goddess's
duty, so Manet's
Olympia is walking
home from the office
job now and thinking
she's a blues singer
huskily whispering,

"and wit' dese
legacies I see
who gon' speak
for me?" and no one
no less a myth
begins.

Chris Gilbert: An Improvisation

The writing on the half-filled helium balloon says,
"Get Well Soon." A few days from getting out of the hospital,
I'm trying to make the balloon float again
while I watch the body of Lt. Col. William Higgins somewhere
in Lebanon swing from its noose on the TV news.
High on Cyclosporine, Prednisone, Imuran, Nefedipine,
Zantac, Tenormin, Lasix, and Persantine, I toss
the balloon on its tether toward the tepid air
around the TV where Dan Rather's voice rises,
though it is as cloaked in lifelessness as the corpse
it describes, which, even as it swings, is getting
hardened into a media thing, a factual because
it's no longer filled with the ponderous void that living brings.
A weight fills me as I allow myself to think
that being alive is hard work, full of just this
human future which, in the light of Higgins, hits me
as an emptiness I make promises of to lift my spirit with.
As I watch TV I imagine the kidney I've been given is
Higgins's, but now my nurse comes in with more medicine
and juice to swallow this with, and stories of how her shift
has been, and promises of a backrub later that, though
it might not show what will become of me as it really is,
does distinguish my next few hours or so from his.
So for this moment I take this strange white setting
and its alien equipment, my nurse, and even my new body
and its present distinctions as parts of a momentary thing
pursuing its momentary meaning, or else—like Higgins—
hardening into a loss or ending. I am reaching to get through
the frozen doors of these stagnant facts, to sully the present
happy affliction with lack, with becoming, or some
unfinished act to show the consequences of where I'm at.

So tonight when the team from hematology troops in
to take my blood again, asking if I'm the transplant patient,
and I go mum because I've gone through this twice
daily now for two weeks, my family who will be
visiting and who will have helped me into whatever
state of mind I am will clear the air for me to declare
I am. The IV unit with my name and directions for my care
taped to the top will indicate I am. The ID bracelet
I've been wearing since I got here will say for me,
"I am." The scar the surgeon left as a signature
on my belly's right side will say, "I am." I am
I feel a gathering possibility passing from temporary
articulation to articulation the way the horizon
arises in the sun as a series of evident illuminations
while the earth spins clockwise toward futurity.
When the time comes I'll rise and say, "I am."
I'll gather all my questions, step into their midst
and say, "I am." I am I am.

Metaphor for Something That Plays Us:
Remembering Eric Dolphy

Memory, you made-up map of presences,
awed attention mending itself into record
which becomes a world worked out inside us. You make
my nature a dressed-up feeling which grows on the given
today and on the hunger of the horizon ahead
which we fill more or less with an act, act
which is not shallow but flute breath's fluttering down
all blue notes and the eighties' longing where I walk
through a park of Dutch diseased elms, the early death
a generation ago of Eric Dolphy on my mind.
When a young bird's plaintive cry—an evanescent
burst from the chest—asks that I hear its singing,
my eventual breath is seed while what's going on
in the trees becomes a belief that the rustling of
the leaves is an expression for. Everything becoming
backdrop, even the traffic at the corner
up ahead in the future where the park ends
mimics a chorus humming at full stop.
Listen. Hear how the meaning of each moment is
the dialect gained when the future assumes the flesh.
I traipse through trash thickets where
the acting president's civil wrongs have trickled down.
Humming what bits I can of "Out to Lunch,"
by the time I get to a bench at the park's edge
where the traffic's strict metronomic
thickens to bicker against the music
in my head, I feel sick—my route afflicted
with the day's euphoric waste that I must fight
else it fills me to the quick. But listen,

even the righteous tire of trying to get it right.
The way we'd like to be like that pure interest, like
that wild witness who uses the caustic specs
of this false nature but is not a victim of the mess.
Bold, absorbed bystander! We made Dolphy into that,
and where did it leave him. So out of this world,
a bothered god in his music, against the lavish nothing
mass-produced by the orchestra of indifference.
That was not his what-is-here, a striving
thing standing beside himself in light of the times—
bud, breath, beautiful momentary being—
a demo of the striving. Undoing
the definition of the diatonic scale, or
displaying his life as a voice, his only future
was to invent a language where he became
his own name pouring from the mouth of his horn.
So much the music in this human world
he never had an audience, never
found another who could talk back.
Man we mess it all up! We step forward
into our urban selves all faithless and lie
as though a presence is a paint job, a fashion—
that put-on face which has its moment that
then, like an uncoded character left
in the oblivious weather, simply fades away.
Feathers will be falling off Dolphy's face
forever; so there is something being said.
Here's a songbird's call, a flute's bent plea,
melts into wail, gathers to pour from
the mouth of the teenager who, I will say,
has come to this park to be

alone because it all feels wrong at home.
I walk closer to the traffic's noise
and see my face in the driver's seat
in a Chevy streaking away from me, and
in this instant it seems that none of this—
the bird's cry, the flute's plea, the runaway,
Dolphy, this passing moment, or I—
amounts to more than a picture
splintering here into dust and time,
where each blue feeling is like a word's
sound when it is read to no one.
Yet when I remember Dolphy I am
aware of myself humming a set of notes
whose sequence tells a story that I become
avowal for. Just as, out of attention,
when you say these words I am brought
to mind, the practice of the tenderness
you have become a witness for.

·~ III. INTO THE INTO

The witnesses are old things, undimmed,
dense with the life of human hands.
    —*Czeslaw Milosz*

Turning into Dwelling

Lord, am I ready? The crickets' sonic party clicks
deep in the grass outside in same tired dying tick
meting out a statistic that does not jump the awful gap
of now. The edge of the window is a groove
that the wind quivers through, making a music—
each note death or a map of destiny.
The midnight is a limit past which I must reach. Invite me
to be part of it. I will not wake and not sleep
unless I can be the language that is this time, words
which risk enough to read and sing to let me come to be
the unmapped footsteps of this summer night come down.

Everything is before me now. It arises all the way
from the walk from the sea to the last sound said
in my tongue. As another seed in which
the most forsaken responsibilities rise up assuming
a place—West Africa, Black Alabama, anthems
of the rueful survivals of the urban Midwest, all
the clotted truths in my blood are loud with those throngs.
The hopes and fears of the screen door's clack in the wind
are a calendar with pages as real as the clock's
click. I turn them to the cadence of the mission
my father left me tucked in the nut in his heart.

The dark July night is a fluid spreading
throughout every minute of me. It is my continuity.
But ghosts are always out there, Lord.
The newspapers are filled with tales of those more
ripe than me who are frozen as a passing note in history—
knives, gunfights, the viruses of fate itself, everywhere
the evidence of this inescapable disease that leaves

the temporary survivor wailing on his hardened knees.
I have made it to my early middle age. The duty
that you have passed to me at every page
is to get those dead into my life, and then defy them.

Now the weariness of race, not the transcendental tears,
now the Black man's blues and booze and reeling with a fate
so fucking hard you're best to sometimes shuck it,
now the thrown-up hands and the laugh about everything,
and the flight from it all with a faith that takes on nothing—
Hellhound on my behind, catch me further on down the line.
Statistical bullets in the air, hide my soul away in prayer.
Lord, the anguish of my Black block rises up in me
like a grief. My only chance to go beyond being breach—
to resist being quelled as a bit of inner-city entropy—
is to speak up for the public which has birthed me.
To build this language house. To make this case. Create.
This loving which lives outside time. Lord, this is time.

Signature

Dear Listener, let the body speak
for itself. The debris floating at this hour,
parts petaling down in the future score
what's been flowering on the street.
The squealed saxophone note is being
adept to its experience with the wind
and its colored cry bewilders the vacant ear
of the expert who declares

it has been silent all these years.
The fresh peas on the antique plate, the swayed
wisteria overwhelming you, the screaming made
with no target in the vicinity—
each thing ad hoc autobiography
in the life it endeavors to be.

"If you aren't there yourself, you
can't bring anyone with you."

—Erica Jay Lippitz

Into the Into

What made the day turn out this way
with me at home singing along "That's How
Strong My Love Is" with Otis Redding on my radio
seconds after hearing the hourly news segue way into
a story on the strip searches Boston's finest do
against every black male in Mattapan old enough
to have the cultural balls which signal "I've got
nothing to prove" and not "forgive me" to
the man who is mauling him or to that other boil—
this business of someone else's order taking over,
without the song in me turning sour
and into an otherness, the willing in me
turned around into refusal, unless
sorrowfully I were involved in living
truths of two kinds: the one—a hard,
staticky particular for this world,
the other—pure and musical, but an image
removed where it romances the phenomenal, where
without the fuzzy frustrations of this world
it can will prettily through my mental heart?

Like moments, they were lined up at the housing office. I don't
mean that there was desperation, but only that they were home-
less and they knew what was expected of them. Whatever was
asked of the first in line, her part in the system was to say, "I'm

next." She was waiting, waiting, just anticipating something she would never, never possess. The end of time. A little tenderness. A corridor where I you he she all line up and the door to the inner room opens up, where the moon comes out when the sun goes down and the ground turns transparent.

.~

What did I do to deserve this
Had my trust in god
Worked every day of my life
Thought I had some guarantees
That's what I thought
At least that's what I thought

.~

"Shattered dreams are a hallmark of mortal life" was written in black spray paint on the storefront window. "Shattered glass is the trademark I make to mend my life" was written on the glass on top of that. Then the kid who is reading this throws a brick through the glass. He say, "my presence on your presence." He say about the glass, "a hole is nothing more than the sum of its parts." He say, "catch me if you can," but it won't be easy. He'll dart underground when you try to catch him, go into subcity, dark dens of duality, confusions and misuses whose meaning can be understood only from the midst of the moment.

.~

Time is a form through.
History as the world's music
scribbles through the skin.

.~

Who is it who is the real Public Enemy,
is it I, the professor, who would
wrest my lines into the here and now of a local lie
good for a few neighborhood blocks and this
false need for a black meanness, mean enough
to knock the game socks off those purveyors of
ironic taste who want a vision metered out
between the lines ruled by the appetites of the wrong
music, which would dress all my neighborhood's wild right
rhymes in tennis whites and proper formalistics,
or is it simply another literal example of
life unfolding in its ugly statistics?

⁑

Form, the historical
host. I don't understand
his opaque list of things.

⁑

Like moments, the souls were lined up at the housing office. I
don't mean that there was desperation, but only that they were
homeless and they wanted back in the world. Whatever was asked
of any one at any point in the line, her part was to say, "I'm next."
She was waiting, waiting, just anticipating something that would
happen to her. The end of time. A little tenderness. A corridor
where I you he she all line up and the door to the inner room
opens up, and she walks in and is in her heart. A room where
the moon comes out when the sun goes down it is a sign. She has
found a name for now.

⁑

The neighborhood kid is lost
Somewhere ahead of him
is his self, a form where
his real growing up is running
its course, a caressable future—
this dark stream overflowing its banks.

Fixing to step into the flow
of traffic, he tiptoes risking
like a tightrope walker
the curb in front of each house
as if his heart were asking,
"is this my true address?"

When, at last, he tries to speak
he lets the nothing come out.
So he comes to feel he's not here
because his nature is cut
and the blood runs into deserts—
a world with Orange County kind of features
and a world which has Watts in it.

⸱⸝

People live everyday
off the waste and decay,
the discards of their fellow man.

Here in Subcity life is hard . . .
please give Mr. President
my honest regards

for disregarding me
for disregarding me.

⸱⸝

This is August 1, 1989, another excuse for pining,
and I have a dream where I am a meaning
that lives longer than Martin Luther King.

In my dream poetry is need
because it reminds me of the junkie who does nothing but hang
in his mute beauty on the corner down the street.

The man wears a sign that says he is *The Living Truth.*
The man is mute except he says he has an emptiness
inside where responsibility lies.

When I open my eyes the world is a TV screen
where I see the meaning starved funky physical teens
hiphop in the latest hundred dollar pair of jeans.

Forgive them, father, for they know not who
their fathers are it is said the living truth said, a prayer
bleeding through his clenched teeth even while he was being beaten.

At the end of the selfless music Frank Morgan is
thanking the listener for saving his life.
The Chambers Brothers sing "Time Has Come Today" again.

I lost track of things when the DJ said, "Well,
it's 5 o'clock rush hour, let's just let
the rhythm get us and let's get a little jungle-y."

"Someone is messin' with yo' image"
was the thing the truth struggled to say.
When I heard that it wiped me away

because he made clear the terror between form and
property and property and form. I have this fear the
formalists are landlords who have rules they want to rent.

When the broken man finally spoke he let in
the terror of property. He said he had nothing to lose,
he said all property belonged to the state.

Now there is a talker going on about the earth as a living
organism. I walk over to the TV screen to wipe him away
with my son's dirty disposable diaper, but he's on the radio.

Now the man is completely mute. Since he has no answers
the truth lets a man possess property
but denies any meaning to the word.

In the blue light of my dream Martin Luther King was saying
you can say anything you want about my dream
as long as I can change the station.

In the context of my dream I look for a word whose
use doesn't indicate otherness as in subcity but gift
as in a process that is alive. This is the other subsidy:

I guess I'm lucky to be alive
I guess I'm lucky to be alive

Some fast furious acts to end a decade of addictions—
doing up food, sex, booze, god, drugs, anything to fill
the "no" inside where the loss of living resides.
Some fiction to fill the selves—sweet deceitful satisfactions.

⌐

He thumbed through his old Beatles albums last weekend and
played them once again. He tuned his radio to the oldies station
and called in a request to have the DJ play something featuring
The Moody Blues. He got out his old Joni Mitchell T-shirt and
took a deep breath to close the final button on his old Levi's and
set off with the wife for the Ben & Jerry's Newport Folk Festival.
He almost always experiences a genuine buzz there, a moment
where he felt nostalgically alive. I would mislead you, however, if
I said all these events were all sweetness and light. You do have
to put up with a powerful lot of preaching and not all of it goes
down as smooth as Ben & Jerry's. The truth is that since for-
eign values were held up as primary role models, many blacks,
through no fault of their own, lost touch with their selves. The
article in *Essence* went on to call Buppies the cream of the com-
munity. One passage stood out, however, and made him wonder
if it was a typo—where the writer asked himself whether to be
one thing for the world and one thing for yourself, if you don't
soon begin to swallow the lies.

⌐

I hear about it happening to others—
living, but I never understood it
(not in the way the day occurs
to me when I meet it
like when I meet the fuchsia I see

while strolling down the street
—purple particulars fusing into
asterisks of new attitudes in the air
like meanings I either choose
to recognize or refuse)
till it happens to me—a present
so mysterious there is and isn't
the possibility of aesthetic refuge,
so what I am involved with seeing
can't be put off
as simply subject matter. So this is
the day, as good as any other
for that which is at my hand—
putting away the poetry and making
breakfast for my son—
first things first, the order
the starting the world over.
So the understanding that goes down
on either side of my door
is not some thought about which
I may or may not be deluded,
but my responsibility, a
living that comes from within
the performance of the incidents
in life, my self included.

     ・ー

The idea of beauty is being there without being there. Models let
operators be there without going there. The models operate at a
distance, they are strictly speaking not robots, but teleoperators—
referring to the fact that that their operation is directed by a

person at a distance. You forget where you are. One appeal of teleoperation is that it allows an expert to work in a dangerous setting while staying safe.

·◡

It's like you're looking
in a window of a house
nobody lives in and I'm
looking at you from the house
across the way . . .
you go and pack your sorrows
trash man comes tomorrow,
leave it at the curb
for time to take away

·◡

The caller criticized the Gaia hypothesis as a model of misdirected responsibility which wants us to believe that the earth is a living being, a neighborhood, with the power to regulate or right itself when things go wrong. It's said that Ralph Abernathy said to a dying Martin Luther King, "It's going to be all right. It's going to be all right." It is not said whether he said, "when." The circuits were overloaded. A spark jumped between the various signs. An undiluted blues filled the August sky. It was futile to deny it. The trees slumped with that sorrow that says SORROW. Barbara came into the house and told the girls to close their windows because it was going to rain. I wiped the stains from my glasses with one of Robin's dirty disposable diapers so I could listen to the talk show caller as she pointed out there was no safe way to find out whether the earth was a vulnerable organism or not.

She and I have a recurring argument about something similar to this. I'd keep wanting to assert the "I" as strong and resilient, to glory in my vigorous, physical existence. I wanted to believe the same about the world, but now I can't remember why. Maybe for myself it was the way I kept seeing things as just appearances but not real, but only through mustering strength could I gesture enough steps in the sensual hiphop of here and now to come to the justice of the real thing. My mind is wrong. The circuits are overloaded. A tear clouded my eye. Why is it that seeing ahead is so messy. I thought I was going to cry. Twenty years after his death we started to mourn Martin Luther King. I had a dream. The facts are all there, buddy, the host said. Check it out. There is nothing to do but to let it happen. But you must gesture like a motherfucka because you're involved in the change.

.⤳

This is the myopic legend happening.
This is a pledge allegiance.
This is the sound of an ethic broken
and then broken again and again.

In a vacuum, maybe, Aristotle
and Ann Landers and Emily Post
and Spike Lee are each right, each self
its shimmering single thing. Each proclaiming

nothing, but how to beat the tom-tom
with the right band and to the right
tune and the right time and in
the right way and with the right hand,

nothing, but the tom-tom's treasonous beauty—
the absent sound of air filling a volume
where you fashion yourself into another thing
so whatever it was you will become, yourself
increasing to the point where you can say we.

᠊ᢛ

"Who's that making that noise?"
Robin asks me.

It is the subject
of the line,

or, as Marvin Gaye sung,
"What's Goin' On?"

The question not as question,
but a moment, a response.

᠊ᢛ

I looked in his drawer for the model,
but found instead a map of a moment.
It was a case of counting the occurences
on the radio station when the DJ mentioned
"responsibility" and "criminality" together
during the weeks of the last year of his presidency.

In the legend was an explanation
for the high count
where responsibility occurred with morality.

The peaks were a picture of the border
to another year and another country.

·‿

A goal, god. A noble need
giving everything a meaning,
that absolute where even the weed
is part of a larger local singing.
That this song isn't pure
doesn't break the voices into facts
empty of that being in the future
where all the loose fragments connect,

no, but it breaks us into nothing
and the fashion which is the present.
Nothing could be the end of history,
but no one lives there. As for me,
the being through what each moment meant,
I'm beyond need I'm one, content yearning.

·‿

Say, get own up and dance to the music.
Get own up and dance to the music.

·‿

i am the meaning
in the word, an image
looking for its time.
if I don't say it
you won't see my story.

i am a passing thing
in which i am a subject—
read my lines, be my mind.
i am absolutely
the I in the writing,
the dead refuse to sing.

          ·⤸

Well, I don't know what will happen now.
The moment is waiting, waiting, just anticipating.
She is dancing to the side of me, going my speed, deliberately.
She is a face rounding my shoulder that I want to turn to face
    before that other voice hustles her away.
This time I've got to save her. To give her chase. To try
    a little tenderness. To woo her with my own word that wails.
    But now she's almost gone. Still she's shouting back
    from the bittersweet beauty of her depthless body. A song.
    I give her chase and, suddenly down her path, what was
    calling her is calling me. All the world that I've ever wanted is
    real through her: the nights and days of small talk and
    coffee, the sexual shudders, the intense longing that keeps me
    sobbing silently to myself, the instants of intuitions
    as clear as math, the answerless world beyond words.
I realize I can't save her but for the moment I grasp her
    garments and through their bittersweet transparency see all of
    living and dying come to be garnered in the image in front
    of me.

Well, I don't know what will happen now.
The moment is waiting, waiting, just anticipating.
She is dancing to the side of me, going my speed, deliberately.

She is a face rounding my shoulder that I want to turn to face,
    before the dis-voice hushes her up.
    Her features in the flux,
the depthless moment
at midnight by the lake, her body just night-grass backbone
in sky farback and air untied.
I lower my sex, heart, being,
and the one sense connected with seeing, the "I" into,
into the sacred canyon
of her who spreads so wide around me—
and in that doubt pawing her,
wondering how many lost others pawing before me,
I wonder in the timeless who
the fuck I am
                (I hate)
                in this moment of face—
less distinction flesh turns sour,
                no selfness
till she who carries this Mambo of darkness
lifts her six veils to the great abyss
brings me to shudder beginning,
till with body burning I flower and hold and kiss
the fazed trust in her local mouth,
till from the midst spills
the truth between us—
blood, neighborhood, words, dream—
this steadfast imaginary community.

Well, I don't know what gonna happen now.
Someone stop this little pain in my heart.
I done looked over, and I done seen the promised land.

I may not get there witcha, but I wanna rock witcha.
I been lovin' you too long, I don't wanna stop now.
I can't get me no satisfaction, but I think I can. I think I can.
Well, I wanna rock witcha.
Well, I may not get there witcha, but I think I can. I think I can.
But it just don't matter with me now. Well, I don't know
    what gonna happen now. There's some hard days ahead. But
    it really doesn't matter to me now. Keep on pushin',
    baby, shake. I think I can. I think I can. So
    I'm happy tonight. I'm not worried 'bout nothing.
Well, I don't know what will happen now.
But I think I can. I think I can.
But I could not, would not, where terror reigns.
And I will not, will not, need useless things.
Not for a Porsche, nor the status quo.
They are not why I'm striving so.
Not for the gain of celebrity.
Nor to suffer more misery.
Not next year. Not quietly.
Not "over there." You watch me be.
Well. We can't face history by looking at a model. At some point
    you have to sacrifice yourself. Coltrane's quest was
    to kill the self, then find it.
Well, we face the mysteries by living among them.
We wouldn't, couldn't, make our way out of history. We make
    our way by way. By making history. Well. So I may not get there
    with you. But.
Well.

Notes and Sources

I "sampled" and paraphrased liberally to make several of the poems in this manuscript. Several of the sources sampled are so well known—e.g., Dr. Seuss—that they need no acknowledgment. The use of some authors is, on the other hand, so indirect that at this point they have become a part of my language. Still other sources, however, are drawn on somewhat straightforwardly and, though their use may be less obvious, they require some form of citation. Therefore, I am grateful to:

Langston Hughes for lines in "The Wall."

Otis Redding, Tracy Chapman, Robert Hayden, Brian C. Jones (of the *Providence Journal*, August 1, 1990), A. B. Spellman, Jackson Browne, and Sylvester Stone of Sly and the Family Stone for lines in "Into the Into."

C. G.

Acknowledgments

Across the Mutual Landscape:

Grateful acknowledgment is due the following periodicals where these poems, or their earlier versions, first appeared: *The American Literary Review, Beloit Poetry Journal, The Black American Literature Forum, Dark Horse, The Little Apple, Mother Jones, Nimrod, Obsidian, The Runner, Small Moon, Sunbury, Telephone, Tendril, Umbral Magazine, Virginia Quarterly Review*, and *The Worcester Review*.

The author would like to express his gratitude to the Massachusetts Artists Foundation for a 1981 grant.

Chris Gilbert: An Improvisation:

The poems included, some in different forms or with different titles, were printed in the following: *African American Review, The Breath of Parted Lips: Voices from the Robert Frost Place, Callaloo, City River of Voices* (*Anthology of Urban Poetry*—West End Press), *The Colorado Review, Crab Orchard Review, Graham House Review, Gulf Stream Magazine, Hanging Loose, The Illinois Review, Indiana Review, Massachusetts Review, Painted Bride Quarterly, Ploughshares, River Styx, Shooting Star, Urbanus, The William & Mary Review*, and *The Worcester Review*. The poem "Blues/The Blue Case against the Lack Of" was first previewed as a performance piece at the Grove Street Gallery (Worcester, Massachusetts, 1985). The poems "Andy Warhol's Marilyn as Nigger" and "Society's Heroic Underdogs" first appeared as part of an exhibit entitled *Art Against Racism*, held Spring 1991, by the African American Studies Department at Brown University and the Langston Hughes Center of Providence, Rhode Island.

Afterword

The summer after Christopher Gilbert died, Barbara Morin, his partner, gave me boxes of his poems and papers to carry back to Indiana in my car. It may have been two boxes—file size, banker's box size, though one had once contained Florida oranges. I discarded one broken-down box, or maybe two—I can't remember for sure—for a couple of empty printer-paper cartons I scored at work. They now reside in my upstairs guest bedroom closet, until someplace claims Chis's papers.

We didn't shed any tears, Fran Quinn and I, as we rifled through the boxes—although the mildew made Fran's eyes water. But we grieved. It was a long process of trying to construct, or to reconstruct, the manuscript we thought Chris had intended. Of trying to reconstruct Chris himself.

Damn, Fran would say every now and then. *He's going to hear from me when I see him again!* (Fran has a deep religious faith.) *I'll let him know what he put us through!* He could have been talking about the manuscript in its many versions, the poems themselves in their many versions. Or he could have been talking about Chris's dying. We understood it was both. It took us a lot longer than we expected to get through it. A year, two years. A long grieving. A sorrow that we touch again every time we talk about this book, about Chris.

We touch joy, too, and laughter—good memories of being young and in love with poetry and with each other as poets, when poetry bound us together in mutual support and served too as a lifeline, one that it seemed might rescue us in a way we had only dimly, desperately dreamed as working-class kids from Lansing, Michigan (Chris), and Clinton and Worcester, Massachusetts (Fran and me).

Chris lived deep in his own thoughts. He was not the easiest person in the world to talk with or to get a straight answer from.

Once I asked him, as a psychologist, to tell me the meaning of a dream I had awakened from to find that I had torn the shirt I was wearing right down the middle. *It means you're a very sound sleeper,* he said.

We reveled in the poets who came to Worcester to read in those days, the seventies. Anne Sexton smoked and fiddled with the gas jets in a science amphitheater at Worcester State College. Denise Levertov fanned our anti-war and political leanings. With Robert Bly we waded into the deep image. Etheridge Knight. Michael S. Harper, Muriel Rukeyser, Lucille Clifton, and Audre Lorde raised our consciousness about race and gender. As a part of a program sponsored by the WCPA, Chris worked in the schools with Harper. Later, the three of us—Fran, Chris, and I—took part in a workshop taught by Levertov. Mary Bonina was there, too, along with John Hodgen and others included in WCPA's Master Poets/Apprentice Poets program.

Recently I came across a poem Chris brought to the Levertov workshop, one that didn't make it into *Across the Mutual Landscape* or into the current manuscript. It was "and the children of the king don't sing," and it referred to Martin Luther King, Jr.'s assassination. It was one of Chris's early poems, dense and opaque. I went back to look for it a week ago, and it has vanished. Did I only dream I'd found it?

In 1984, *Across the Mutual Landscape* was published, and so was my book, *The Persistence of Memory*. We celebrated with a book-signing party at Don Reid's Ben Franklin Bookstore. What an occasion that was! The synchronicity of our lives in those days still amazes me.

The manuscript we chose to call *Chris Gilbert: An Improvisation,* after one of the poems, contained many poems we had read before, often in several versions. But there were new poems, too, or poems so heavily revised, reconstituted, expanded, and rearranged that they were essentially new. It's not that Chris's poems ever became easy. Never easy, either in content or in craft. They became, if anything, more intense, more ambitious. They deepened, and the reader plunges into them, into the deep rhythms of Black experience, Black speech, Black music, and Chris's thoughts. He had a sense of mission and purpose in his poems. He spoke for himself, but he spoke also across time, to and for those who came before and those to come. One poem in the new collection that especially moves me is what has become the title poem of this book, "Turning into Dwelling." Here is the final stanza:

Lord, the anguish of my Black block rises up in me
like a grief. My only chance to go beyond being breach—
to resist being quelled as a bit of inner-city entropy—
is to speak up for the public which has birthed me.
To build this language house. To make this case. Create.
This loving which lives outside time. Lord, this is time.

Chris had a keen sense of time. He seemed to know his own time was short. We retained the subtitle he had given the collection: *Music of the Striving That Was There*. Despite kidney disease, a transplant, and serious illness leading to his death, he never stopped striving to create. He never stopped improvising.

—Mary Fell

Christopher Gilbert was born in Birmingham, Alabama, in 1949, and grew up in Lansing, Michigan, the fourth of six children. His parents and several of his siblings worked in General Motors assembly plants, as did he during summer vacations. Gilbert received a BA in psychology from the University of Michigan in 1972 and a MA in psychology from Clark University in Worcester, Massachusetts, in 1975.

In 1977 Gilbert cofounded, with Etheridge Knight, the Worcester Free People's Artist Workshop, which he also led from 1977 to 1981. He was active for many years in the Worcester Poetry Association, and he was the recipient of two fellowships from the Massachusetts Artists Foundation in 1981 and 1989, and a poetry fellowship from the National Endowment for the Arts in 1986. His first book, *Across the Mutual Landscape*, won the 1983 Walt Whitman Award from the Academy of American Poets, and was published in 1984 by Graywolf Press. He was Poet-in-Residence at the Robert Frost Place in Franconia, New Hampshire, in 1986.

Gilbert was the editor of the short anthology *Something Else: A Sample of Writing from Third World Writers*, published by Dark Horse Magazine in 1981. His poems and essays have been published in numerous magazines and in several anthologies, including *The Morrow Anthology of Younger American Poets*, edited by Dave Smith and David Bottoms, and *The Jazz Poetry Anthology*, edited by Sascha Feinstein and Yusef Komunyakaa. His poem "Any Good Throat" is installed in granite at the Jackson Square stop of the Boston MBTA subway system.

Gilbert worked as a psychotherapist in a variety of settings, including the University of Massachusetts Medical School Counseling Center, the Judge Baker Guidance Center, and Cambridge Family and Children's Service. He taught writing classes at

Goddard College, Worcester Polytechnic Institute, the University of Pittsburgh, Trinity College, and Clark University. He began teaching psychology at Bristol Community College in Fall River, Massachusetts, in 1993, a position that he held for the remainder of his life.

Gilbert is the father of two children, Robin, born in 1987, and Gracie, born in 1994. After a twenty-year battle against the complications of polycystic kidney disease, he died in 2007.

Terrance Hayes is the author of five collections of poetry, including *How to Be Drawn* and *Lighthead*, winner of the National Book Award. His honors include a MacArthur Fellowship, a Guggenheim Fellowship, and a Whiting Writers' Award. He teaches at the University of Pittsburgh.

Mark Doty, editor of the Graywolf Poetry Re/View Series, is the author of nine books of poems, including *Deep Lane* and *Fire to Fire: New and Selected Poems*, which won the National Book Award. He is also the author of five books of nonfiction prose. He teaches creative writing and literature at Rutgers University and lives in New York City.

Turning into Dwelling has been typeset in Berling, a font design by Karl-Erik Forsberg in 1951 for the Berlingska Stilgjuteriet in Sweden. Book design by Wendy Holdman. Composition by Bookmobile Design & Digital Publisher Services, Minneapolis, Minnesota. Manufactured by Versa Press on acid-free, 30 percent postconsumer wastepaper.